ROUGH ROAD TO FREEDOM

A Memoir

Neil T. Anderson

MONARCH
BOOKS
Oxford, UK & Grand Rapids, Michigan, USA

Published by Monarch Books
an imprint of
Lion Hudson plc
Wilkinson House, Jordan Hill Road, Oxford OX2 8DR, England
Tel: +44 (0)1865 302750 Fax: +44 (0)1865 302757
Email: monarch@lionhudson.com
www.lionhudson.com

ISBN 978 0 85721 294 8
e-ISBN 978 0 85721 388 4

A catalogue record for this book is available from the British Library.

Printed and bound in the USA.

"Neil Anderson's gifted insights into the reality of spiritual warfare scratched an itch and brought healing that had eluded the mainstream church. *Rough Road to Freedom* will be an inspiration, a book that helps one understand that the victorious Christian life has already been procured by Jesus Christ and is ours for the taking."

– Jerry Rankin, President Emeritus, International Mission Board, SBC

"We have always been grateful for being part of Freedom in Christ Ministries… Neil is a man of integrity, living out his freedom in Christ. We're sure the Lord looks at Neil's life so far and says, 'Well done, good and faithful servant.'"

– Jerry and Sally Friesen

"Neil and Freedom in Christ Ministries have impacted all of us in Community Bible Study. We are so grateful for the way our Lord has used Neil to help equip us as servant leaders. I highly recommend this book: it summarizes a lifetime of walking in obedience to His will and purpose. You will grow spiritually as you read these biblical principles lived out to His glory."

– Camilla L. Seabolt, CEO/Executive Director of Community Bible Study

"Our lives have been forever changed by the road to freedom that Neil took. For years we have witnessed first-hand in Asia the liberating power of the message of freedom in Christ. It is thrilling to read how God used the experiences that shaped Neil's life to bring forth the transforming message of freedom to so many people around the world."

– Dr. Rick and Laurel Langston, East Asia School of Theology, Singapore, and Campus Crusade for Christ

"A truly inspiring story that reads like a movie script, and yet it's real and true. This testimony of a life transformed is a must read."

– Arnold J. Enns, President of COICOM

"Neil Anderson's life journey – as he discovered the truth that sets people free, and learned how to communicate this to others – will inspire you."

– Colin Urquhart, founder of Kingdom Faith

"*Rough Road to Freedom* chronicles biblical insights about our new identity as children of God. My friends and patients have been renewed in their faith as I have shared what I have learned from the many FICM resources."

– George A. Hurst, MD, FACP, FCCP, Director Emeritus, University of Texas Health Science Center

"This book is a jewel. We catch a glimpse of the man behind the movement, and praise God for the remarkable fruit that resulted. Whenever God's people implement his biblical teachings with genuine repentance, authentic faith and diligent follow-through, the lasting results are remarkable!"

– Chuck Mylander, EFM Director

"Inspiring and challenging. Neil's rediscovery of these biblical truths – of truth encounter and our identity in Christ – has changed and liberated countless lives spiritually and emotionally, and transformed my perspective and my practice of spiritual warfare ministry. You will be enlightened and blessed by Neil's story."

– Dr. Paul L. King, Associate Professor at Oral Roberts University

"I have used Neil's Steps to Freedom in my teaching at Liberty University, and I have outlined his steps in my writings. Praise God for Neil Anderson's contribution to the Christian church, and for his awesome ministry."

– Dr. Elmer L. Towns, Co-Founder and Vice President, Liberty University

"So many counselors deal only with symptoms, but Neil helps us find healing for the causes of emotional and spiritual problems. His memoirs show that he did not write from an ivory tower, but from the context of his own participation in the battle in which we are all engaged."

– Dr. Timothy Warner, Former Director of Professional Doctoral Programs, Trinity Evangelical Divinity School

Contents

Dedication and Acknowledgments

I want to thank Tony Collins, and Monarch Books, for believing the message of Freedom In Christ Ministries. Tony has been an invaluable support to Steve Goss, our United Kingdom Director and now the International Director. Because of his support the message has spread to thousands of churches in the UK and around the world.

Freedom In Christ Ministries would not be what it is today if it hadn't been for Jerry and Sally Friesen, who were the first to come alongside and help me. Jerry saw that the ministry in the States was incorporated, and served as the first operations officer. Ron and Carole Wormser were essential to the ministry and traveled with Joanne and myself for years. Their many years of experience were a great contribution to the ministry. The same is true for Tim and Eleanor Warner, who helped spread the message around the world. When we needed Ron and Carole's input at the home office, Hal and Alandra Parks stepped forward and traveled with me for years. Robert and Grace Toews took the message to Canada, where it has spread throughout the land. The ministry is indebted to their contribution, and those who follow will stand on their shoulders.

When this book is published I will have completed forty years of service and be 70 years old. It is time to pass the baton to the next generation, which is why I dedicate this book to our international directors:

Rich Miller has co-authored books with me, and directed our United States office for many years. We first met when I was doing a conference in the Philippines, and Rich was on staff with Campus Crusade for Christ. Rich caught the vision and brought a rich devotional spirit to our team. He is a genuine peacekeeper.

Clay Bergen became our Canadian Director when the Toews retired. For seventeen years he has faithfully taken the message all over Canada. Clay's major contribution to our International Council is prayer. He makes sure that we stay connected through prayer.

Victor Manogarom came out of retirement to be the Director in India, but that was only to help set up his son Isaac. Isaac is our networker, and had to grow up fast when Victor passed away. He and his wife Tara also have a "Steps" home for abandoned children, which reflects the nature of their hearts.

Roger Reber is our Director in Switzerland, and he was handed the ministry when the previous director became ill. Roger has a remarkable testimony of God's grace. The police had to rescue him from a very dysfunctional home, and Roger knows how to empathize with those in despair. He also has many technical skills to advance the ministry.

Bob Genock has been a gift from God to me for the last few years. Bob retired from Xerox and traveled with his wife to Holland as missionaries where he discovered our ministry. After he lost his dear wife to a brain tumor I asked him to help me with international ministry. Only then did I find out that most of his professional career had been in Latin America, and that he spoke fluent Spanish. He became our Latin American Director, and my traveling buddy when we went south.

Steve Goss was our United Kingdom Director, and he has now become our International Director. Steve and his wife Zoe have been a model of consistency. In ten years Steve has developed teams throughout the United Kingdom and introduced our ministry to thousands of churches. Several European countries now have representatives for our ministry under his leadership. I have always been a message-driven person, but Steve has the talents, gifts, and vision that are necessary to expand the ministry.

Finally, I thank God for all those who represent our ministry throughout the world. Many labor in obscurity and sometimes alone. But they know who they are in Christ and have seen God set people free, and no one is ever the same after that. May God bless all of you, and reward you greatly for being faithful.

Neil T. Anderson

Foreword

A little before noon, Stanley Johnson entered our one-room country school and told the teacher to send the children home, and to leave herself. Stanley was the farmer who lived closest to the school and a school board member. The forecast looked grim. A "northerner" was moving in faster than expected and the county roads would soon become impassable. Such winter blasts could come suddenly and engulf prairie communities like ours with high winds and heavy snows.

Normally my sister Peg and I would walk the mile home, but this storm had taken us all by surprise. So the teacher drove us halfway home on the county road. We would have to walk the last half mile on the township road. Such roads were sparsely graveled, barely more than a lane wide, and maintained by the farmers who made up the township. Nobody would clear that road until after the storm, and then only after they had plowed the lanes that connected their own farms to county or township roads.

We were experiencing a "white-out" when the teacher dropped us off. It didn't have to be snowing that much for visibility to be less than a few feet. Howling winds would blow the snow across the plowed fields and gather in the ditches that lined every road.

Our Scandinavian ancestors had settled this rural community and planted groves of trees on the north and west sides of the farmyards. They provided some shelter for the livestock that huddled in the barns, hog houses, and chicken coops. Much of the snow would collect in the groves, but enough got through to make large drifts that had to be cleared in order to do our daily chores.

My grandfather had immigrated from Norway and settled that farm. He was more of a carpenter than a farmer. He built most of the buildings on our farm as well as the school that my father attended, as did I, my brother and two of my sisters. My father was born in the patched-together house that I knew as home for twelve years. His mother died at his birth, which created a rift between him and his father that was never repaired. He was sent to live with his grandparents in Iowa who spoke only Norwegian. When my grandfather remarried, my father was brought back to the farm around the age of six and had to learn English in the country school he attended until his eighth and final year of education.

My sister and I barely made it home that day. Peg got sick from the intense cold and threw up, but we struggled through the snow and blinding conditions that made it almost impossible to see where we were going. Mom and Dad were greatly relieved to see us trudging through the snow. We were frozen to the bone. Life wasn't easy in those post-Second World War days. My father had been exempt from the draft because he was a farmer, but also because of a bout with polio that had left one leg shriveled. He was to lose that leg in a farm accident when I was little more than two years old. That was my earliest childhood memory, seeing him in that hospital bed.

We were poor by today's standards, but we didn't know it. In hindsight we were rich in other ways. I truly cherish my childhood.

I was raised in a community where neighbors looked after one another, and family was the bedrock of our culture. There would be no money to help us kids with our education, but that didn't stop us. Paul, the eldest, would complete his doctorate and do post doctoral work at Tufts University. He taught at the University of Minnesota Medical School in Duluth, Minnesota, for thirty plus years. Shirley, my elder sister, would finish nursing school. Peg, the fourth to be born, would finish a master's degree in sociology, and be intimately involved with Freedom In Christ Ministry. My youngest sister, Alice, would finish her doctorate in education.

I was the fun-loving and adventurous one of the bunch who never took school too seriously. Nobody, including myself, would have predicted at the time that I would eventually go into ministry, complete five degrees, author or co-author sixty books and be the founder of a ministry that has spread around the world. This book is about a couple called into ministry, who struggled to grow through the trials and tribulations, as every child of God is called to do. It's about the rough road to freedom that Joanne, my wife, and I have traveled to be where we are today, and the lessons we have learned along the way. I still wonder, "Why me?" I certainly did not plan this amazing adventure.

Somewhere on this fascinating journey God put a burden on my heart to see captives set free and their emotional wounds healed. First, I had to discover who I was in Christ, and allow God to guide me through a lot of paradigm shifts. My early education was steeped in western rationalism and naturalism. It has taken me years to discover the reality of the spiritual world, and to learn to be guided by the Holy Spirit. It was even more difficult to learn how to overcome the evil one and to believe the truth that the whole world lies in his power (1 John 5:19). I have gotten beyond denominations, and sense no obligation to defend any systematic theology. I am just a child of God serving Him in His kingdom. Over the years I have heard people say, "I can't peg you." To which I respond, "Try 'Christian'."

I had no early plans to go into ministry, although I can look back and see little seeds that were sown along the way. I wanted to be a farmer, but God had something else in mind. I served in the Navy before completing my degree in electrical engineering. I worked as an aerospace engineer for four years before I sensed a call to go into ministry. I was a high school campus pastor, a college age pastor in a large church, and an associate pastor before I was a senior pastor. I had no ambition to be a seminary professor, but that was my job for ten years. I thought I had found my life's work at the seminary, but God led me to start Freedom In Christ Ministries.

I have never advertised or sought to market Freedom In Christ Ministries. I have never sought a position in ministry. I have never gone where I haven't been invited. I have never tried to raise support for this ministry, or charged for my services. All my individual counseling has been free. Freedom In Christ has offices around the world and many representatives, but doesn't own anything. We raise our own support, and rent our facilities. I will not spend a minute of my time to keep this ministry afloat. I believe parachurch ministries like the one I founded are meant to come and go. The Church, however, will remain until the Lord comes back, which is why I remain committed to the local church. Our purpose is to equip the Church worldwide so they can establish their people, marriages, and ministries alive and free in Christ through genuine repentance and faith in God. As a ministry, we exist to help others and their ministries to become more successful.

As I share my own journey of discovery, I pray that it will

strengthen your faith and equip you to be an instrument in His hand to set captives free and bind up the broken-hearted, which is what Jesus came to do. May God truly bless you in your own journey toward fulfilment in Christ.

1

Learning to be Trustworthy

Life was simple on the farm. Nobody owed you a living so you worked hard. What we planted in the spring determined what we harvested in the fall. Farmers inherently know that what they sow they shall also reap (Galatians 6:7). Cause and effect were built into the system and that left an indelible impression on my thinking. Presenting problems have a precipitating cause.

My father's wooden leg affected our whole family. Until the accident he had been the most ambitious farmer in the community. He had been the first to buy a combine which cut the grain and threshed it in one operation. He not only tilled the family farm, he rented other property, which he had to let go after the accident. He fed cattle, but that had to stop since it required more manpower than he could manage. So he gave up cattle and started to raise sheep. My brother and I were the beneficiaries and we alternately became the "lamb kings" of Jackson County.

All summer we groomed our lambs and showed them at the county fair. That led to many blue ribbons and occasional trips to the State fair. I looked forward to the county fair as much as I looked forward to Christmas. More than once I stayed the night sleeping in the pen with my lamb. Next to the fair grounds was the town's swimming hole. It was fed by an underground spring so it stayed fairly clean until the "dog days of summer." Usually by August they had to close it for health reasons, but that didn't keep us from climbing over the fence and doing a little skinny-dipping after dark.

Dad's handicap also affected how he raised us. I became "his legs", and when he told me to run and get a tool, he meant run. If I walked after that wrench it would be best if I just kept walking that day. I learned obedience through the things I suffered, much like someone else I know (see Hebrews 5:8). I also was the one who had to go in to stores and ask questions on behalf of my father. I learned to take the initiative at an early age and not to feel embarrassed to ask questions when I lacked understanding. Dad was a taskmaster and I learned from him how to work and take orders, but I didn't learn much from him about how to live with or relate to others. That I learned from my mother.

My mom lost her mother when she was nine. Her father immigrated from Sweden and settled into our Scandinavian community. Her mother was half Scotch-Irish. She taught my mother those good old Irish songs and Mom sang them to us on the farm. To this day I love those old Irish songs. When my grandmother died, my grandfather hired a Canadian woman to be his housekeeper and to help with the children. Later they married, which turned into a difficult situation for my mother. Partly to escape a dysfunctional home, she married my dad before she completed high school, and became a farmer's wife. Married at seventeen, she had four children by the time she was 23 years old. (My youngest sister, Alice, was born thirteen years after the fourth child.) Mom knew how to cook and sew, but as a new wife she had to learn to plant a garden and preserve the vegetables and fruit for the winter. That was what we lived on from fall to spring each year.

After harvest we spent every weekend cutting wood for the furnace that heated our home. By midnight the fire would go out, and Mom would get up every morning and start a new fire in the basement furnace. There was no heat in the upstairs room where my brother and I slept. In the winter we would take hot water bottles to bed with us to warm the sheets and our feet. One night my bottle slipped out from under my sheets and froze solid. There was frost on the inside walls of our room. The most dreaded task my brother and I had in the winter during lambing season was to take turns waking up in the middle of the night. Someone had to see if a lamb had been born during the night. If it were lying too close to the wall it would likely freeze to death before morning. We had to put the lamb in a pen with its mother and place a heat lamp over the newborn. Returning to that frigid room and bed that was no longer warm was painful. We had an occasional fight over whose turn it was.

Social life was centered around 4-H and church. 4-H is a youth organization administered by the United States Department of Agriculture (USDA). Their mission is to engage youth to reach their fullest potential. The name represents four personal development areas: head, heart, hands, and health. We had monthly meetings at the local township hall, which had a small meeting room and kitchen. It was great. We sang, played games, and planned yearly events, which included our own softball team that played other townships. My brother was the pitcher, a position that I later assumed. The big event every year was the county fair. A couple months before the fair we all caravanned to each other's farms, and saw their gardens and the livestock that would be shown at the fair.

Dad was raised Lutheran, but Mom was the spiritual leader and we attended the Methodist church she was raised in. There was a processional every Sunday morning with the choir singing, "Holy, Holy, Holy, Lord God Almighty…" On one particular Sunday morning while the pastor was delivering his sermon I recall thinking, *I could do that.* For some totally unknown reason, when the choir and pastor did the recession that morning, I got up and followed the pastor out the door! Mom was shocked and asked me why I had done that. I said, "I don't know." It just seemed like the thing to do at the time!

I'm thankful for all the Bible stories I heard and the wonderful potlucks I attended. I can't remember a time in my life when I challenged the credibility of the miracles and events depicted in Scripture, and I have always thought of myself as a Christian. Only years later did I discover that I wasn't. If the gospel was preached, I never got it.

The little country school had seasonal events that other family members attended. One Mother's Day we acted out the play Hansel and Gretel. I was in the third grade and the narrator. I was supposed to say that Hansel and Gretel went into the heart of the woods, but the "h" in heart came out an "f" – quite by mistake. That made it a memorable Mother's Day for the mothers, but not for me. Even though I was generally the life of the party and the consummate jokester, I had trouble standing in front of people. My eyes would water and I struggled to maintain any composure. Two events changed that; one was helpful, the other not!

The first was in my seventh grade. I had just started attending school in town. At first I was a little intimidated – being a farmer's son and coming from a one-room school in the country. Most of the students had been raised in town and they already knew each other. It didn't help that upon my first entry into my homeroom I tripped over the doorsill and fell on my face, to everyone else's delight. However, two weeks later I was elected class president. I was by nature a socially inclined person in spite of the pratfalls.

That fall my brother, Paul, and I were champion and reserve champion of the Western Lamb Show. The Jackson Junior Chamber of Commerce and the Kiwanis Club honored us with a luncheon on Monday at noon. I carried my hand-me-down suit to school with me on the bus and changed before the luncheon. I sat to the right of the mayor of this small country town and tried my best to cut through the toughest Swiss steak I had ever encountered. Suddenly my knife slipped and my left hand that was holding the steak in place with a fork cleanly left the plate and implanted itself on the white table cloth between myself and the mayor. The retreat to the plate was just as speedy, but it left an unmistakable mark on the cloth inches from the "significant other." Somehow he kept a straight face.

Paul was introduced at the luncheon and said very little, other than to emphasize that he was just the reserve champion and the one they wanted to hear from was me, the grand champion. My eyes were already moist and what I really needed was the bathroom. Somehow I got through my speech, but nobody was overwhelmed, except me, and not in a positive way. My proud mother was watching in the wings, but my first public speaking event offered no promise of my becoming an orator.

In the eighth grade, my homeroom teacher persuaded me to

enter a speech-giving contest. Why I did, I have no idea. It certainly was not my natural inclination. The speeches had to be memorized and given after class one afternoon. To my astonishment I actually won, even though four of my friends were standing outside the door making faces at me and laughing their guts out. There was a stiff penalty for winning. I had to give the speech in front of the whole student body. How much of life is providential? How much do I owe that teacher for helping me get over one of the biggest hurdles in my life? I never struggled with speaking in front of people again.

Our school had a program called "religious day instruction." Every Tuesday afternoon the classes were shortened, and for the last hour we could go to the church of our choice. It wasn't forced religion. Students could go to the study hall if they wanted. I went to the church of my mother's choice! But one warm fall day I decided to skip the class and went to the park with a friend. I came back in time to catch the bus, and went home thinking that I had gotten away with it.

I did not. On Wednesday morning the junior high principal called me in to his office and chewed me out. This man was scary. He even looked like Hitler, with his beady eyes and mustache. He finished his lecture by saying, "I've arranged for you to be off this Thursday and Friday." I was shocked. Expelled from school for two days, because I skipped religious day instruction?

I was not looking forward to going home that evening. Alternative plans were forming in my mind. I considered getting up on Thursday morning and pretending I was sick for two days. Or I could get up, do my chores, pretend to catch the bus, and then hide in the woods until it was time to come home. I knew my sister would rat on me so I had no choice. I had to face my parents, but I was not looking forward it. Approaching one's authority figures when guilty is a daunting prospect. In my case I knew who to approach first: that would be my mother. There would be some mercy in her presence.

So I said, "Mom, I have been expelled from school for two days, because I skipped religious day instruction." Her countenance took on a strange look and then a smile broke out on her face. "Oh Neil, I forgot to tell you. I called the school yesterday and asked if you could be excused Thursday and Friday to help us pick corn." I could have gotten away with my indiscretion, but God arranged it so there would be no secrets between me and my parents.

If I had known that Thursday and Friday's absence from school was excused, would I have dreaded going home that evening? Of course not. In fact I would have run up the lane and joyfully approached my parents. That whole experience was so much like our relationship with God. The apostle Paul wrote, "Therefore, since we have been justified by faith, we have peace with God" (Romans 5:1 ESV), and "There is therefore now no condemnation for those who are in Christ Jesus" (Romans 8:1 ESV). Too many Christians live as if they are walking on glass, afraid to make the next step lest the hammer of God should fall on them. The hammer has already fallen. It fell on Christ. He has already died for all our sins. We are not sinners in the hands of an angry God. We are saints in the hands of a loving God who has called us to come before His presence with confidence and boldness (Ephesians 3:12 ESV), and with our hearts sprinkled clean (Hebrews 10:22 ESV). Such insights about our relationship with God would come years later.

After my eighth grade, everything changed. My father saw the handwriting on the wall: when he saw his eldest son go off to college he knew that farming did not hold a good future for him. In the middle of lambing season, which was in the dead of winter, my mother and father made a trip to Arizona. They left me in charge of the farm. The house was the responsibility of Shirley, my elder sister. They came back three weeks later and announced that they were going to rent the farm to a neighbor and move to Arizona after the school year. It jolted me out of my comfort zone. To this day there is an image in my mind, planted as we drove away from the farm. My sister Peg and I were on our knees in the back seat looking out the rear window and watching our dog chasing after the car. Slowly he disappeared out of sight, never to be seen again. Mom and Dad had visited Arizona in February when it was pleasant, and now we were moving there in June. For the next four months the daytime high was never lower than 100 degrees. I thought we had moved to hell.

Dad had no job, and no particular trade skills. However, every farmer that I grew up with was an electrician, plumber, carpenter, painter, welder, roofer, and mechanic. Dad worked at odd jobs that summer until he landed employment at Air Research as a mechanic. He kept that job for twenty years and hated every minute of it. Dad had never taken orders from anyone other than the father he despised, and he winced every time the whistle blew signaling a crew change. When the opportunity presented itself for him to transfer to the night shift, he took it. The night shift gave him some respite from daytime supervisors, and the white-collar workers left him alone.

However, there was no way my Dad would let his son to sit around all summer. So I worked as a migrant farm worker that first summer in the Arizona heat. I picked onions and water melons for most of that summer. I did wonder why I was the only white kid out there. At the end of one row were two cream cans of water for drinking. I walked over to one and took the ladle for a drink, only to get it knocked out of my hand by the foreman. "That's for coloreds," he said. That was my first exposure to racism. I grew up in a Scandinavian community where racism was playful bantering between the Norwegians and the Swedes. I asked my parents about it that evening and they had little to offer in terms of insight. Racism was new to them as well. At the end of the week, I got paid in cash as my brothers, and when I got home it just went into the family coffer. I had never been paid to work before and, anyway, it didn't belong to me. It belonged to the family. Farm boys didn't get paid for working in those days. It was just expected of us. It was part of our chores. People today would probably call that child abuse, but I didn't think it was.

At the city swimming pool I stood in line waiting my turn on the springboard. Some Mexican boys jumped in front of me and that really riled my fairness factor so I challenged the one who cut right in front of me. Next thing I knew I was outside the swimming pool facing-off with a Mexican boy surrounded by many others who were not rooting for me. I think that was my first fistfight with another person, and it was my last. The fight was a draw, but it left me longing for Minnesota.

My mother took a couple of night classes and finished her GED (General Equivalency Diploma), and applied for a position in a bank. Two years later she was the operations officer. My mother could have been anything she wanted to be, but she chose to be a servant. At the age of eighty-five she was still volunteering for hospice, making calls on "old people" and shut-ins. There was a lot she could complain about, but she never did. I have always said, the good you see in me is Jesus and if there is any other good in me it is my mother.

I struggled in Arizona. It wasn't home to me. We joined another Methodist church and that was an OK experience. No conversion took place, but I found friends and some social outlet. Still I longed for Minnesota. After my sophomore year I asked my parents for permission to go back to Minnesota for the summer. I had made enough from a morning paper route to pay for a one-way ticket on a bus. At the end of the school year I left on a two-day trip with $10 in my pocket. After driving all night we stopped at a bus depot, and they gave us enough time to eat breakfast. I was hungry and I piled my plate full in the buffet line. It came to over $7 and now I had less than three dollars to last for the next day and a half.

The bus stopped at Fairmont, Minnesota, which was thirty miles from Jackson, my hometown. So I took my suitcase, walked to the highway and stuck my thumb out. The third car picked me up and, remarkably, the driver lived three doors from my uncle, which is where he dropped me off. It had been arranged that I could stay with his family until I got a job. I had no idea what my prospects were at the ripe old age of fifteen. I called my childhood friend, Ronnie Fransen, at the first opportunity I had. He was surprised to hear my voice. Two hours later he called back and said I could work for his uncle that summer and live with him and his family.

That began one of the best experiences of my life. Ronnie's uncle, Russell Fransen, and his wife Merva had two young daughters, but no sons. Russ and I bonded that summer. In many ways he became the father I never had, and I was the son he never had. We arm wrestled, raced each other and worked like dogs. I attended the Lutheran church with the family. I loved every minute of it.

My own father believed that his father blamed him for his first wife's death. I never knew my grandfather, because he died in a car accident before I was born. Everything on the farm where I was raised spoke of my grandfather, but I never heard my father mention him until Dad was 75 years old. When he did, he just said, "That man!" in disgust. The only other time was when Dad was about 85 years old and he said, "That man should never have had children." It is painful to know that my father remained bitter all those years. To my knowledge he never forgave his own father. By the grace of God I did forgive my father, but I have often wondered why his bitterness didn't have more of a negative impact on me than it did. It think it affected my sisters more than it did me. To me, Dad was like a tough boss and life was OK if I obeyed him, which I did. I always had my mother to go to for advice and sympathy, but my sisters would receive no emotional support from their father.

I believe there is another reason why I was not embittered. I grew up in a close farming community. There were so many other men around that I could, and did, look up to. They always liked me, and I looked forward to the times they came over to help us, or when we went to their farms to help them. But more significant were Russell Fransen and his brother Teal, who farmed together. They were great role models.

At the end of that summer Russell and his family drove me to Colorado Springs where we spent the night and saw the sights. The next day they put me on a bus and I went back to Arizona.

In my junior year I tried out for the varsity wrestling team. I had put on some muscle that summer and I was ready for the contest. The team captain was also in my weight group and I could beat him, or at least wrestle him to a draw, but the coach let him wrestle at that weight which was 154 pounds, because he was a senior. I could try out for another weight, but I couldn't beat the two guys at 165 or 177 pounds so I tried out for the 191-pound weight group. That is the weight I wrestled at in my junior year and I won half my matches even though I weighed less than 160 pounds.

The most memorable match of my life, and the one I recall and feel the best about, was our match at South Mountain High School in Phoenix. The man (he wasn't a boy) I was destined to wrestle was an All State center in football that year, and he had won the State championship in wrestling the year before as a junior at the same weight. When we weighed in he had to strip naked to make weight. I could have jumped on the scale fully clothed and the arm wouldn't have wavered a bit. When our weight was called, our team was leading by nine points. Our heavyweight wrestler was a sure loss and destined to be pinned. That would cost us five points. If I got pinned, we would lose the match. If I lost without being pinned, we would lose three points, but the team would win.

I even remember that guy's name. It was Stacy Ostland. When I walked out on the mat, the small crowd of spectators laughed. They laughed! My coach's parting words were, "Just don't get pinned." Hey, thanks coach!

Thirty seconds into the match he made a move that landed me on my back. I bridged for the rest of that period and he never got me in that position again. In fact I scored two escape points on him, which represented two of the five points scored against him that whole season. The team went nuts. In the locker room afterwards, two African American students from South Mountain came up to me and said, "We are so glad that you didn't get pinned, now he won't think he is so hot." That was not the proudest moment I suffered in defeat – that would come many years later.

The following summer my parents let me drive a dilapidated 1950 Studebaker back to Minnesota to work again on the farm. I paid $200 for that piece of junk, and I could write a whole book on my exploits with that car. It looked like a two-row corn picker and you couldn't tell whether it was coming or going. Russ and Merva had had another daughter that winter, so that summer I stayed with Teal and Evelyn Fransen, who had three rowdy boys that wrestled and tussled with me all summer. When the end of summer came, they invited me to stay and help with the harvest. I moved across the road and stayed again with Russ and Merva for the winter. I spent my senior year with them and graduated from Jackson High School in 1960.

Merva left a letter out for me to see that she'd received from my mother. In the letter Mom said, "Take care of my son, he is my favorite." I don't think Mom had any favorites, she just wanted me to believe that. But I cherished that thought and thank her for it.

Living in the United States was different in those days. How many parents would let their child get in a bus with a one-way ticket, travel halfway across the country with no plans in place for when they arrived at their destination? How many would let a 16-year-old boy drive a clunk of a car across the country? I was thinking about this years later and wrote my parents a letter thanking them for trusting me. This trust in me had a profound effect on my life. I wanted to live up to their expectations, but was I perfectly trustworthy? Nobody is, and yet God has entrusted us with the gospel and to preserve the integrity of ministry. That is a challenge I want to live up to.

Living away from home, I could have easily abused that trust, but I didn't want to let my parents down, and I didn't want to let God down. That was one of the biggest lessons of life that I have ever learned. As a parent or a pastor, we can communicate trust or a lack of it. As a pastor I have had parents tell me that one of their children has run away. Usually that happens at about the age of fourteen. When I ask them what they are going to do when the child comes back, you can almost guess what the typical answer will be. A lack of trust is probably why they left in the first place. I have the normal amount of blind spots and character defects, but if you were to ask me what I thought my greatest strength was, I would say, "Trustworthiness," and I have my parents to thank for that.

During that senior year of high school, I talked a lot about farming with Russ and Teal, and they offered me an opportunity to farm with them. Essentially, I would work for them and I could use their machinery to farm the old family farm. That was the direction I was heading until word came to me that my father and his sisters had sold the farm. There was a moment of disappointment, but I accepted it as God's will. Now that the farm had been sold, what would I do?

My brother had just graduated from the University of Minnesota and was working as a grad assistant heading toward a doctoral degree in biochemistry. Although I hadn't taken high school seriously and I had no real direction, that spring I applied for admission to the liberal arts program at the same university. To qualify for admission the university sent an exam to my high school, which I was given a full day to finish. We needed to bale hay the day I was to take the exam, because you have to make hay when the sun is shining. So I finished the exam before noon and went home to work on the farm. Needless to say I wasn't accepted.

So I applied for the school of engineering instead; I always received good grades in math and science without trying. This time I had to take the exam at the university, and I passed.

That fall I enrolled in the school of engineering with the goal of being a chemical engineer. How well do you think that worked out? I left school before the semester was even finished. All my grades went to an F, because I never officially canceled my classes. I did get something out of that failed effort. I met Joanne Espe, a sophomore transfer student from a small Lutheran college. We dated for most of that semester, but when I left the university we parted ways with no commitments, and I joined the Navy.

2

Called into Ministry

I was standing on the fantail of the USS *Leonard F. Mason*, DD 852, buckling myself into a harness. To provide stability the ship was doing only 15 knots. A helicopter was hovering overhead. A line started to descend from the chopper and I connected it to my harness. Slowly they winched me up. As soon as I had cleared the deck, the chopper took off for the sake of my safety. They didn't want me banging against one of the gun mounts. I felt like Peter Pan flying through the air.

Once I was safely aboard the chopper, the pilot returned to the aircraft carrier. I had spent the day aboard the carrier receiving instruction. This was an additional assignment to my regular duties. On board my destroyer, I was a sonar man. I had enlisted for six years to be part of the nuclear training program, which included two years of school. After boot camp my orders were changed, and I was drummed out of the nuclear program because my less than perfect eyesight disqualified me for submarine service. I received the good news that my enlistment was reduced to four years and they sent me off to sonar school. Sixteen weeks of electronics training proved to be invaluable years later.

I attended Protestant services during my time at "A" school, as they called it. One Sunday morning I sensed a call to the ministry that was so clear I even wrote a letter to my parents sharing my thoughts. Was I just a lonely sailor looking for a better experience than I was having in the Navy? Boot camp and "A" school didn't leave me with any warm fuzzy feelings toward the military, and the thought of four more years like that didn't inspire hope. However, life did improve after basic training.

Near the end of sonar school we were given a "dream sheet" in which we could state our preference for duty. Nobody took it too seriously. One sailor thought it was a joke and put in for Guantanamo Bay, Cuba. You guessed it; he got what he asked for. I requested any assignment in the Second (East Coast) or Sixth (Europe) Fleets. I received orders for the Seventh Fleet, a destroyer stationed in Yokosuka, Japan.

Being a naturally coordinated and stocky farm boy, I was the unofficial athletic director aboard the ship. I pitched for the softball team, quarterbacked the football team, and even played some basketball. While most of the sailors partied and drank, I worked out in the gym and, on shore, checked out bicycles to ride around the countryside to take pictures. Recognizing my physical prowess, they assigned me the additional duty of being a "Sea and Rescue Swimmer." If we had a swim call, I was the lifeguard. If the hull needed to be inspected, I was the one to dive under the ship. When we did plane guard, I was equipped to go in the water to rescue the pilot should a plane go down. Plane guarding took place while planes were being launched or landing on a carrier. We were there for the pilots. That is why I was being transported over to the carrier, to receive instruction on how to rescue them from the water. Their major problem was the shroud lines that were part of their parachutes. The umbrella of the parachute would sink rapidly, and if a pilot got caught in the lines he would probably go down with it.

On board the ship I was one of the few who attended church services each Sunday morning. Our ship was too small to carry a chaplain, so one of the officers would lead Sunday morning "worship" services. It was usually less than inspiring. Attending church on Sunday morning had been deeply ingrained in me from childhood. I remember being awarded a pin in that little Methodist church signifying nine consecutive years of church attendance. On board the ship I was known as the "Christian." In the military some would see that as a sign of weakness or the basis for ridicule. Being the unofficial athletic officer as well as the sea and rescue swimmer probably saved me from any derision. I had a few good Christian friends, who really were Christians. I wasn't at the time, but I thought I was.

Being on a ship stationed in Japan had its rewards. I got a tour of Asia. After our assignment was over we sailed back to the States, and passed through the Panama Canal on our way to Boston. Our ship was being retrofitted at the Boston Naval Shipyard. Most of the crew were assigned elsewhere, but I stayed on board. They sent me off to another school that trained me to maintain our new sonar system and I helped to install it.

A friend asked me if I would exchange the night watch for him so he could be home on Christmas Eve with his family. He would stand by for me months later when we stopped at Acapulco, Mexico. It was a good deal for both of us. I stood watch as the duty officer that night and listened to Christmas carols in a little hut near the gangway as it snowed outside. Talk about feeling lonely! Most of the crew were in the barracks. I was one of three aboard the ship. The other two were sleeping somewhere below deck. I was relieved from duty at a quarter to midnight, which gave me enough time to attend the Christmas Eve midnight service at the Old North Church. Dating back to colonial days, it was still functioning as a church. It had original pew boxes and a nice family asked me to sit with them. If I was somewhat depressed when I arrived, I was really depressed when I left. For me, that was a miserable service and I don't even remember why.

After a year in Boston we set sail for the east coast and I got to see the Panama Canal again. As we sailed up the west coast of Central America the Captain authorized a swim call since we were two hours ahead of schedule and the seas were calm, allowing the ship to come to a complete stop. Two men were stationed on the second deck with M1 rifles in case a shark came by (there is always some uneasiness to swimming in an ocean a mile deep with no land in sight). They threw a cargo net over the side for us to have some means to climb back aboard. My assignment was to dive in first and set the outer perimeter. As soon as I surfaced, the whole crew was hollering for me to come back on board. I leisurely swam back to the net and started to climb up just as a mammoth shark swam underneath me! We pulled up the net, steamed ahead for about an hour, and threw the net over the side again. No sharks this time so we got some relief from the heat.

We docked in Long Beach, California for about a month and I heard about an AAU Greco–Roman wrestling tournament that was open to anyone. I thought, *Why not?* So I signed up and attended the clinic that briefed us about the rules of Greco–Roman wrestling. It is quite different from the collegiate free-style wrestling that I was familiar with: you can't use your legs in Greco–Roman wrestling, and each match has two five-minute periods. That style of wrestling attracts those who have a lot of upper body strength, and I might add, stamina. Two five-minute periods is exhausting, especially for someone not actively in training like myself.

I made it to the finals, but something happened to one of my knees in that match. It just popped under the strain, and I had to forfeit. I struggled to get off the mat and take a shower. I returned in time to watch the heavyweight final, but while sitting in the stands my knee froze at an awkward angle. Somehow I got back to the ship, but I couldn't sleep. I woke up one of my shipmates and he took me to the USS *Hope*, a hospital ship at the base. The only doctor on duty was a pediatrician. X-rays revealed no broken bones, but he ordered a cast for my leg. They worked for half an hour to get my leg straight and then slapped on a cast from my ankle to the top of my thigh. Three days later we sailed for Japan.

Try getting around a destroyer with one leg stiff as a board. Our ship not only had no room for a chaplain, it had no room for a doctor. So the corpsman and I tried to figure out why I even had my leg in plaster. We couldn't find a good reason and cut the cast off. Oh, what a relief that was. My leg started to get better, but it didn't fully heal.

That was the fall of 1964 and we were in the Tonkin Bay off the coast of Vietnam. Two of our sister ships, the *Turner Joy* and the *Maddox,* were the destroyers that had sunk the Chinese gunboats that triggered the start of the Vietnam War. One morning I woke up to see the entire horizon dotted with amphibious ships ready to land thousands of soldiers. I was slated to be discharged in December, but they wouldn't let me leave until my replacement came. I could have kissed his feet when he arrived on time. I'd had a good tour of duty, but I was ready to be discharged and get on with my life, and on December, 7, 1964 I received my honorable discharge.

With the military behind me I was now ready for college, and this time I was motivated. I enrolled at Arizona State University to become an Electrical Engineer. To support myself I found a job at Judson High School in Paradise Valley, Arizona, an expensive private school with grades one through college prep. I was a dorm master and their wrestling coach. It was a perfect job since I had the days off to attend college, and it provided room and board. It didn't pay much, but I didn't need it since I had the GI bill.[1]

My knee was still giving me problems so I saw a doctor. He asked when I'd injured it, and I said, "When I was on duty in the Navy." Since I didn't have any insurance, he suggested that I contact the Veterans Administration (VA) hospital. They said I needed surgery and I scheduled it for Christmas vacation when all the students went home. Just before I went to the hospital I received a letter from Joanne Espe. After my first year in the Navy I had felt lonely and had mailed a letter to Joanne. We'd exchanged letters for a few months, and then we'd broken up again, so I was surprised to receive her letter.

Joanne still had my parents' address and sent the letter to them. She was coming to Arizona over Christmas to see her parents who had now moved there. I invited her to come see me in the VA hospital. It had been five years since we had dated. When I stopped the letter writing she'd taken that as an end of our relationship. In the following year she met another man and they'd married. Seven months later he was killed when a private plane that he was piloting crashed. Less than a year after that tragedy she found me in a wheelchair getting milk from a cooler at the VA hospital. Six

1 A bill providing service personnel with financial assistance for college after an honorable discharge.

months later I resigned from Judson High School and we were married on June 4, 1966.

Joanne had finished her college degree with a double major in food and nutrition from the University of Minnesota. Our plan was for her to work to put me through college, and for me to finish my studies as soon as possible. She found a job as a dietician at St. Luke's Hospital in Phoenix. The pay was horrible, but we managed. A year later she was able to get a much better job at Arizona Public Service as a home economist. For two summers she did their live cooking show on television twice a week. Meanwhile I completed 100 semester units in two years and graduated magna cum laude. Engineering school wasn't fun, especially at that pace, but I was sure that degree was the end of my formal education. Little did I know!

I had no interest in joining a fraternity, but I wanted some avenue to play sports. I arranged to be a perpetual pledge with a fraternity so I could play intramural sports. It was a good arrangement for both of us. They could use my high grade point average, and I could pitch for their softball team, swim for their swimming team, and play for their football team. However, while racing around the right end with the football my good knee gave out and down I went. It was time to hang up my cleats and focus on being a good student and husband.

In those days, recruiters would come on campus to hire Electrical Engineering (EE) students. I was doubly attractive since I had military and electronic technician experience. I received twenty-two job offers and never left the campus. One offer was from the Honeywell aerospace division in Minneapolis, Minnesota. So guess where we went? Home!

To buy a house, I applied for a VA loan that required no down payment and we moved into the quiet suburb of New Brighton, Minnesota. Joanne was pregnant with our first child, and we attended a small mission church that met in our neighborhood. Although she was raised a Lutheran, Joanne had converted to Catholicism for her first marriage. Becoming a Catholic was off my radar screen so we compromised and became Episcopalians. We both felt OK about that and settled into suburban living.

Even though I had gimpy knees I pitched for a softball team, played in a golf league, and bowled on a bowling team in the winter. We were the all-American suburban family. Heidi was born on March 12, 1969. Life was good when a spiritually alive Episcopal priest came to our church on a Sunday morning and invited us to attend a Lay Institute for Evangelism presented by Campus Crusade for Christ. I really didn't know what evangelism was. I was content with my spiritual condition and thought, *If you don't knock on my door, I won't knock on your door. You can believe whatever you want, just leave me alone, and I will leave you alone.*

I was senior warden of the church. If you are not acquainted with such terminology, I was chairman of the board. The priest wanted to attend the Institute and asked me to go with him. It was scheduled for five consecutive mornings the following week from Monday through Friday. I didn't have any strong feelings one way or another about going. As fate would have it I was free to go since the computer time I needed at work wasn't available in the mornings, only at night. Engineers typically don't work at night, but that week I did; it was the only week of night work that I ever did as an engineer. So we went to the Lay Institute for Evangelism: we being the priest, Joanne, myself, and Joanne's father, who happened to be visiting us at the time.

It took me two days to realize I was learning to share my faith

– and didn't have any. The definitive question that penetrated my mind was, "If you took Jesus out of your religion, what difference would that make?" I thought, *Ya, what difference would that make? I believe in God?* In hindsight, that is astonishing. My whole ministry today is based on who we are in Christ. On Wednesday of that week they gave an invitation to receive Jesus Christ as our Lord and Savior, and I made a decision to trust only in the finished work of Christ for my salvation. I was born again. For the first time in my life I understood the gospel, and it was indeed "Good News."

At the end of our training on Friday they said, "Don't tell anyone that you came to this conference unless you come back tomorrow and go door to door in this community and share your faith." I went home thinking, *No way Jose. I have come a long way in two days, but not that far,* and Joanne agreed. I wrestled with God well into the night and finally I woke up Joanne and said, "We're going tomorrow." Joanne said, "We are? Well OK, but you have to go with me."

I have never really struggled with fear, but this was intimidating. I was scared stiff, and had no self-confidence to rely on, which is what they wanted. They wanted us to rely on God, and, to ensure that happened, we could not go out in pairs with our spouses. In the next two hours I led three people to Christ. They didn't make a decision for Christ due to my intellectual brilliance and professional skill. They heard a simple presentation of the gospel and responded by faith, which was astonishing to me. The field actually was "white unto harvest." Experiencing that almost had a bigger impact on me than my own personal decision on the previous Wednesday.

I was sobered by the realization that I had played church all those years. I had been just one of the multitude of religious nonbelievers that dot the landscape in America. Everything changed after that. I started to see Christian bookstores that had gone unnoticed before. Christian periodicals and books seemed to come out of nowhere. I started to feel convicted about my speech, and other behavior that I had just seen as "normal" patterns of life. I had a strange and decidedly new burden for my fellow engineers.

Then the unexpected happened. I was offered a job with our plant in West Covina, California. My boss called me into his office and said, "I'm obligated to share this offer that came for you from one of our California plants. Before I share it, I just want you to know that you have job security here, and I personally don't want you to leave." The offer was rather puny – it involved a $100 a month raise and they wanted my answer by tomorrow morning. I went to work the next day and told my boss that I was not accepting the offer, and I thought that settled it.

That evening I got a call from the personnel (now called human resources) office in West Covina and they wanted to know why I had turned them down. They really wanted me to come because they had just landed a $100-million contract to supply the sonar and underwater fire control systems for over ninety frigates that the Navy was building. I told them, "You gave me one night to make a major decision in my life that included a move to a state I don't particularly care for, and to do all that for a $100 a month raise."

There was an astonished pause on the other end, and then I heard, "That was not the offer, and you can have as much time as you want to make this decision." My boss had lied to me. How could I continue to work for such a man? That realization became the deciding factor that God used to help me make one of the most important decisions of my life. Most people would not see a job transfer to California as a good spiritual move, but it was for me. Many Americans think God rotated the world west one night and everything that was loose rolled to Southern California – and I was just one of the nuts who did. In reality, God took me out of my comfort zone and gave me an opportunity to start over again as a new believer.

Joanne was pregnant with Karl, so I put her and Heidi on a plane to Arizona, where they would stay with my parents until I got I got things arranged in California. The company bought my home in Minnesota (part of the offer), paid for the move and put me up in a hotel for a month. We settled in to make our home in the land of fruits and nuts.

We looked around and found another Episcopal church. A few months later Karl was born, and we wanted to have him baptized. Mark was a good Baptist friend who had transferred with me from Minnesota, and I asked him and his wife to be Karl's godparents and stand up for him at his baptism. They came to our home one evening to talk about it and gently shared their belief about baptism. Then they agreed to be godparents and be with us for Karl's baptism even though they disagreed with the Episcopal practice of infant baptism. What a great witness that was to us.

We soon discovered that the priest at the Episcopal church had a lot of personal problems. I was attending a B&B men's study on Tuesday evenings. B&B stood for beer and Bible. The host supplied the first round of beers, but you had to bring your own if you wanted more. Most did, including the priest, who'd started B&B because he was an alcoholic. Then we found out he was having an affair. I shared that with Mark, and he invited us to try his church.

We did try it, and we stayed. It was like I was entering a candy store. I couldn't get enough. I was there Sunday morning, Sunday evening, and Wednesday evening. Everything was new to me and I loved it. The burden for my fellow engineers grew more intense, so I called the pastor and asked what I should do. He suggested that I start a Bible study at the plant. I asked him how to lead a Bible study. My only experience had been B&B! He said, "Why don't you start with the Gospel of Mark. Read a few verses and ask if anyone has any questions. If not, read a few more verses." I thought, *I could do that!*

I visited the personnel office at work and asked permission to use conference room C every Wednesday at noon. He said that was fine. I posted a notice on the company bulletin board: "If anyone is interested in a Bible study, come to conference room 'C' this Wednesday at noon." The announcement was up little more than an hour when Sam Rosen, one of God's chosen people, brought the slip of paper into my cubicle and said, "You can't bring Jesus in here." I said, "Sam, I can't leave Him out." "What do you mean by that?" he queried. I said, "Every day I walk into this building He comes in with me!"

Sam didn't like my answer and he went straight to the personnel office. They called me a little later and said, "We hate to withdraw our permission, but we can't have such a conflict on the work premises." I told them I understood, and asked if I could just put up a notice to meet next door at the bowling alley. They had a small conference room and could even serve us breakfast. So that is where we met.

I was pleasantly surprised to see over twenty men come to our first breakfast. There were several "secret service" Christians, and a couple of Mormons, who dropped out after the first week. The one who surprised me the most was Mort Pate, a Catholic colleague of mine. Mort found the Lord. I have seen many conversions, but then there was Mort. He became an outspoken witness at the plant. A year later when I resigned and left for seminary, he took over the Bible study.

I ended up being the lead systems engineer overseeing the underwater fire control system that our company was responsible for. Sonar was just part of the system. Sonar located the target, but the system also included a missile-setting panel, a main frame computer, and ASROC (antisubmarine rocket). Once the target was identified, a rocket that carried a torpedo would be launched from the ship to the approximate location of the enemy submarine. The torpedo would separate from the rocket and go into an active search mode, spiraling down in a circle until it contacted the sub.

We were nearing the completion of our first production model when I was asked to help conceptualize a new system. A naval research facility in Pasadena had asked for our help. I was given full access to the West Covina art department as the intention was to take our plans to the naval research center. After a month the plans were scrapped and I went back to my design work.

Then a surprise announcement came. The company still wanted the presentation, but not in Pasadena. They wanted to take it to the Navy department in Washington. If that had been the original plan, they would have brought in a marketing expert, whom I would bring up to speed, and he would have taken the proposal to Washington. But time was of the essence, so they called in all their top brass and asked me to make the presentation to them. If I passed the test, I would go to Washington with Harry, our plant president. It couldn't have gone better. The plan was to leave the following Monday morning. Before we left Harry asked if Joanne and I would like to have dinner with him and his wife at their home when we returned. I had to turn him down, because I had already agreed to go to our church's men's retreat the following weekend.

Our trip to Washington was a career-changing success. Harry took me on a tour of Washington and we ate at the Army Navy Country Club. The Navy department was impressed with the presentation. If I was looking to catapult my career to the next level, this was it.

On the plane home, I was reading one of Bill Bright's *Transferable Concepts*. Harry asked me what I was reading, so I briefly shared my new-found faith and what the booklets were. He politely listened, but not for long. He said, "I'm a Unitarian," and then shared for several minutes his beliefs and concluded by saying, "I don't think Jesus was any kind of a god. He was just a good moral teacher."

What do I say? What should I say? Who do I work for? I had read from the book of Colossians that we were to obey our masters, and "Whatever you do, work heartily, as for the Lord and not for men" (3:23 ESV). I had already made up my mind that I was working for God at Honeywell, believing that should make me a loyal employee and a better engineer. It wasn't just a job for me: it was a mission field. Besides, I had just read in one of the *Transferable Concepts* a quote from C. S. Lewis's *Mere Christianity*: "A man who was merely a man and said the sort of things Jesus said would not be a great moral teacher. He would either be a lunatic – on the level with the man who says he is a poached egg – or else he would be the Devil of Hell… He has not left that open to us. He did not intend to."

So I said to Harry that I'd just read this quote by C. S. Lewis and proceeded to share it with him. Essentially I was saying,

"Harry, you dummy, you are wrong." I wasn't thinking that, but that is the message Harry heard. He plugged in his earphones and didn't say another word until we landed. His only comment was an instruction for me to get the luggage and he would get the car. It was a mostly silent ride home, and after he dropped me off we never spoke again until I left the company. I thought I had really blown it.

Two weeks later Harry asked my friend Mark how the men's retreat was. Six months later a fellow engineer said, "I thought you'd like to know something. I was at a cocktail party with Harry last weekend, and he was telling everyone that you were the best systems engineer he has ever worked with." "Harry said that?" I asked, surprised.

Six months later, I resigned and left for seminary. Since I had a top-secret clearance, security had to be with me when I cleared my desk and then escort me to the exit. I had said my farewells to my friends and had only one more door to go through when Harry approached me. "You wouldn't leave without saying goodbye, would you?" he asked. I was speechless. We hadn't talked in a year. He pulled up a chair across from me and said, "We may disagree about some religious issues, but I have never respected anyone more than I respect you." We actually hugged, and I left. In hindsight, I probably hadn't blown it, but it was an invaluable experience for me. Learning to be a faithful witness without regard for our own personal wellbeing is a hurdle every Christian needs to get over. Harry needed to hear the truth and needed to know the Lord, and that was more important than my own personal ambitions.

My biggest blessing at the plant, however, was a man by the name of John Borror. He was a maintenance man who worked in the shop. He was a blue-collar worker and completely different from me, but we connected spiritually. His ministry was to convalescent hospitals. Every Sunday afternoon and Wednesday evening he would teach the Bible to these aging and crippled people. Some probably never heard a word he said as they sat slumped in their wheelchairs.

He invited Joanne and me to his modest home for dinner, because he wanted our wives to meet. We had a pleasant evening of fellowship, and then he asked if I would like to see his library. I said I would, expecting to see a shelf or two of his books. I'm sure my mouth dropped as I entered a room where every wall was lined with books from floor to ceiling. "John," I asked, "how many of these books have you read?" His reply amazed me: "Well, all of them. I don't buy a book that I don't intend to read." I do! In fact many of the books that I have accumulated over the years remain unread. John even read commentaries.

As I was leaving the company, John said that no one had ever been laid on his heart to pray for more than me, and he promised to pray for Joanne and myself for the rest of his life.

Years later, at the end of the spring semester, I heard a message in the seminary chapel that cautioned us to take time off from ministry. I hadn't taken any time off for years. I was working part time at a large church as the college pastor, which meant I worked full time and got paid half time.

That afternoon I told the pastor that I needed some time off and he agreed. He suggested I take the following week off, but with no pay. It was a step of faith since I had no money and the loss of a week's half pay was significant. The next morning the doorbell rang at 7:30. It was the mailman with a registered letter from John Borror. Inside the envelope was a check for $500 with a note that said: "I thought you could use a vacation." God had put that thought in his mind months earlier, and he had agreed with his wife, a real estate agent, that should she sell a house then the commission would be tithed to us.

I had taken out a $1,000 National Defense Loan for my seminary education. With such a loan you don't have to make any payments until nine months after you graduate. Nine months after graduation I received a letter from the government informing me how I could pay off the loan. Two days later the doorbell rang at 7:30 in the morning. It was the mailman asking me to sign for a registered letter from John. Inside was a check for $1,000 with a note saying: "For your education." John had no knowledge of that loan. There was also a $50 check made out to Joanne. I had made it through seminary without Joanne having to work thanks partly to the GI bill. Since I had finished engineering school in less time than usual, I still had two years of eligibility left. I wanted Joanne to stay home with the children and I believe that little check for Joanne was confirmation that what we did was right.

John came to my ordination and sat on the back row with tears in his eyes. He always wanted me to get my doctorate and years later when I did so I sent him a note. Within a week I received a letter from his wife informing me that John had died. I was shocked. How come I hadn't heard that? I was moving the week before Easter to take a position at Talbot School of Theology. John was so much like Christ that I wasn't surprised that he died on Good Friday! They were trying to contact me to do the funeral, but I was unreachable.

I have had the privilege to meet and work with Christian leaders all over the world. Most were godly men and women, but none of them seemed more like Jesus Christ to me than John did. He was God's gift to me at a time when I really needed to know that Christian leadership is not about titles, degrees, diplomas, and social status. It is about godly character and credibility. I decided that when I "grew up" I would like to be like John, who was just a simple humble man who heard from God and obeyed.

Meanwhile, back at the Baptist church we attended while I was working at Honeywell, I heard about EXPLO '72. Campus Crusade for Christ was inviting young Christians to go to Dallas, Texas, and meet for a week in the Cotton Bowl, a 100,000-seat football stadium. I told my pastor that we should encourage the young people in our church to go, and I was willing to provide the leadership. He thought that was a great idea and said he would support me 100 per cent. I realized later that meant he would pray for me.

I chartered a bus that could transport forty-two people and challenged the young people in the church to go with me to Dallas, Texas. Three weeks before we were to go, three people had signed up. I was discouraged to say the least. However, three weeks later, forty-two of us boarded the bus for Texas. Bill Bright, the founder of Campus Crusade, said at the beginning of the week that on Thursday evening he would challenge us to go into full-time ministry. That evening he asked us to stand if we were ready to make that commitment. I think I was the first one that stood up. Joanne said, "What are you doing?" I said, "I don't know!" I asked her to stand up with me, and she did. A month later I resigned my position at Honeywell and off we went, with our two children and a dog, to attend Talbot School of Theology, a graduate School of Biola University in La Mirada, California.

3

Forgetting What Lies Behind

Word got out that I was heading to seminary, and the local director for Youth for Christ invited me to have lunch with him. He said there was an opening to be the club director at a local high school. Most of his staff were part-time students and they had to raise their own support. He offered me the position, and said a businessman had offered to support me for $200 per month. I had no concept of raising support or desire to do it, so I took the position.

Having just left a profession that required great precision and quality control, I was about to enter a ministry of organizational chaos. I was ready to resign after the first staff meeting, but I thought I would give it one more chance and attend their annual August staff retreat in Palm Springs. The hotel rates are pretty low at that time of the year, but the temperature wasn't. It was more organizational chaos, and that just about put a nail in the coffin. Then Jay Kessler, the President of Youth for Christ at the time, gave the final talk. I was impressed, and that persuaded me to be a club director during my first year at Talbot School of Theology.

The power of influence can't be overstated, and it is a power that must be wielded carefully. Jim Allen was the only reason I chose to attend Talbot. He was the associate pastor in the Baptist church we attended, and taught the young marrieds class. I was impressed with him as a person, and the only one I consulted about seminary education. I could easily have been influenced to attend any number of schools. God must have been watching over me, because I am thankful for that choice to this day. I also chose to pursue a degree in Christian Education, since that is what Jim had done. Only God could have known that I would be teaching at Talbot ten years later. I had no such ambitions.

First year seminary students can easily be caught up in idealism. The body-life movement was sweeping the country. The church wasn't an organization. It was a living organism. In addition, the charismatic movement was gaining momentum. Neither typified our Baptist church; our pastor was staunchly against the charismatic movement and he was an organizational man if there ever was one. He was one of the few pastors that I have ever met who had the gift of administration. He was well organized and had a plan to reach our city for Christ. The church grew rapidly under his leadership. He had a plan to knock on every door in our community. Tragically this go-getter was to burn himself out and die of cancer at the age of fifty-one.

One day I played golf with the music director at the church, who taught at a Christian college. On the first tee I asked him what he thought of our pastor. As he was addressing the ball, he said, "Frankly, I can't stand the man!" For eighteen holes I only heard about the pastor's character defects. Those bitter little seeds of judgment were in my mind every time I attended church. Besides, his style of leadership did not fit the ideal church that I was learning about in seminary.

The pastor railed so much against the charismatic movement that I decided to check it out myself. The largest church of such persuasion was holding a charismatic clinic, which I attended with Joanne. Although it was a strange experience for me, I couldn't see anything that was decidedly not Christian. I left with a neutral position and was content to let time be the judge. To this day I appreciate the wise counsel of Gamaliel, who cautioned his fellow Pharisees not to act too hastily in their opposition to Jesus, saying: "for if this plan or this undertaking is of man, it will fail; but if it is of God, you will not be able to overthrow them. You might even be found opposing God" (Acts 5:38–39 ESV)!

By the end of my first semester my heart had turned bitter toward the pastor. I couldn't stand the man. At seminary I was being taught to love and forgive. I tried, but with little success. Finally I told Joanne that I had to go see him. A root of bitterness had sprung up in the church and many were being defiled (see Hebrews 12:15), and I could no longer be a part of that. So I called him and asked for an appointment.

I must have appeared slightly nervous (I sure felt that way), and he asked me to sit down. Then he came around the desk and sat in a chair opposite me. "How can I help you?" he asked. I couldn't delay this any longer and said, "I came to ask your forgiveness for not loving you." There it was, I got it off my chest, and we talked for another hour. To show you what kind of man he was, he offered me a position in the church. Philosophical differences prevented that from happening, but a profound healing took place in my soul and we remained friends for years to come. (The music director ended up having an affair and lost his marriage, as well as his position at both the university and the church.)

My experience with Youth for Christ was a mixed bag. Nationally and internationally they were and remain a great ministry. One should never judge the whole ministry by one of its parts. Locally at that time, the primary financial base came from the infamous "haunted house." The leaders would find some old dilapidated house and turn it into a horror chamber. Kids would pay money to have the living daylights scared out of them. I couldn't have any part of that, but I wanted to be loyal to the organization, so I asked if I could set up a display at the end of the frightening tour, which is what I did. One young lady looked at the material and said in surprise, "You're a Christian organization?" I said we were and she responded, "Then why are you scaring the hell out of me?" Now there is an entry for a gospel presentation!

Other staff opposed the idea of having the haunted house as well, but our director kept doing it because it had become a major part of the ministries' financial support. I made a personal decision from that experience. I would never let money or the lack of it be the basis for ministry decisions. I would never compromise my convictions for financial gain, and I never have.

On the positive side I learned a lot about campus ministry. One night I gave a talk about sex, and a young man who came with his Christian girl friend asked, "I'm not a Christian, but if I had sex with my girl friend, would I regret that later on?" What a mature question! Another young man thought abstinence was a joke, and he saw nothing wrong with pornography. I asked him if he subscribed to something like *Playboy* magazine? He did, so I challenged him to try something. When the next issue arrived in the mail, I asked if he could put it by his bedside and not look at it for a week. He said he could do that, so I offered him a gentleman's bet (no money) that he couldn't. He said, "You're on."

I didn't see him again for several weeks until one afternoon while visiting the campus. He saw me right after I saw him and tried to duck away. It didn't work, and I asked him where he had been and reminded him of the bet we had. I asked him if he had been able to wait a week before looking. A day? An hour? "It was a stupid bet," he said. "You know," I said, "I wouldn't take that bet myself. It is unwise to put ourselves in a position of temptation like that. Besides, what you think is the freedom to look, I think is bondage, because you can't keep from looking." I left it at that.

In my first year at Talbot, the Billy Graham ministry produced a film entitled *Time to Run.* Their plan was to show it in public theaters, and give an invitation at the end. I signed up to be a counselor, but somehow ended up being the counseling coordinator. Somebody must have thought I was mature enough to do that, being a seminary student. Little did they know. This was breaking new ground for me. At the end of the film, Billy came on the screen and presented the gospel. My assignment was to pick up the microphone and invite people to come forward. As far as I knew, that had never happened before in a public theater. The first night the theater was packed, and I was praying with my counselors in a back room. I left early to be fully prepared and properly stationed at the front of the theater.

Actually I wasn't early. Our timing was off by several minutes. Billy Graham was finishing his lines just as I was coming through the back door. I raced to the front, picked up the microphone and asked the people to remain seated. Many were already in the process of getting up. Big beads of sweat were forming on my forehead, as people stared at me in unbelief wondering, *is this guy for real?*

In a Billy Graham crusade, hundreds of people get up and start coming forward after Billy gives the invitation. Initially they are all counselors. That primes the pump. Seeing people going forward gives the fence sitters courage to get up and go forward. Suddenly, after what seemed like an eternity, the back door opened up, my counselors saw what was happening and hurried to the front. A herd of people got up and followed them. Somewhere around 125 people was way too many people for fifteen counselors to talk to individually.

With my best Billy Graham impression I told those coming forward that their family would wait, they just needed to come. I had no choice but to lead them through a sinner's prayer as a group, while family and friends looked on in utter disbelief, or exhilaration and every other emotion in between. I was so excited that I floated home in my pastoral limousine, which was a Volkswagen Bug.

The next morning at seminary I had to tell everyone what happened. One man seemed to be totally unmoved by my presentation, so I asked him if he had seen the movie yet. He hadn't seen it, so I asked him if he was going to see it. "Probably not," was his response. "Why not?" I asked. "Because it is being shown in a movie theater." I stared at him in disbelief. I had never heard of anything like that. I had no previous exposure to old time fundamentalism. I didn't even know what legalism was. I told him that they didn't serve liquor there and the popcorn was safe to eat, in fact downright enjoyable. It didn't make any difference.

There were still some trappings of that at Biola University when I first attended, and Talbot was part of their University system. To be accepted I was asked to sign a commitment not to be involved with the naughty five: dancing, drinking, smoking, movies, and cards. I couldn't sign that. My family played cards every time we got together, and there was no way that I could go home for Christmas and not play cards. So the Assistant Dean called me in to his office and asked me why I hadn't signed the pledge. When I explained my position, he said OK and signed me off. "By the way," I asked, "what is wrong with playing cards? Is it gambling?" He really didn't know and said, "I think it has something to do with the figures on the face cards."

Such indefensible standards can kill the church. In such settings one can be bitter, hate, steal, be divisive, and still be OK – just as long as you don't dance! Thankfully, such thinking was long gone before I came back to teach, or I couldn't have returned.

The Baptist church I attended had some similar rules, which were probably left over from the prohibition days. To be a church member you were supposed to pledge abstinence from any kind of alcohol. I just ignored it and I suspect most of the others did as well, but my hypocrisy did bother me a little. I was never a heavy drinker, but I did enjoy a beer on a hot day. Besides, I couldn't find any biblical basis for total abstinence. In fact, the apostle Paul suggested that Timothy take a little wine for his stomach, and Jesus turned water into wine at the wedding feast. That was enough biblical justification for me to continue having a beer now and then, when there were no Baptists around.

Shortly before I moved to attend seminary I bought four cases of beer on special and stacked them in my garage. Then something strange happened to both Joanne and myself. A conviction came over us and we realized that we didn't need to consume any more alcohol. Joanne emptied her wine bottles in the sink. She never drank more than one glass at a time anyway. It didn't seem right to pour out the beers however, so they just sat in my garage. When four friends from church came to help us move into an apartment, I gave them each a case of beer for helping me, and let them sort it out. When conviction comes from God, the power to stop comes with it.

At the time I had two obsessions that needed to be dealt with. One was bridge. At Honeywell, I played in a bridge club every noon at work. Duplicate bridge can be very competitive, and frankly I was good at it. I could tell you on Friday every hand that was dealt on the previous Monday. Most of the other engineers could as well. Engineers are an interesting breed. The problem was, it had become obsessive. Some of the guys would go on bridge cruises at sea and play day and night. Two were Life Masters, which is quite an accomplishment. You have to win a few tournaments to get that rank.

The other obsession was golf. Four of us at the company played every Saturday morning. One of us would get up Tuesday morning around 4:00 a.m. and stand in line at the golf course in order to get a good tee time for Saturday morning. We were a competitive group. I never swore or threw clubs, but I thought about it a lot. It was only fun playing if I played well. One of the four was Jewish by birth, and he had a foul mouth. One day it really got to me and I said, "How does it feel to stand with one foot in the gutter and shout profanities all the time?" "Does it bother you?" he asked. I said it did, and he toned it down.

I heard a simple message that changed all that. "How do we know the will of God?" asked the evangelist. "How do you know whether something is right or wrong when the Bible is silent about the subject?" he queried. I remember two of his three points as clearly as though I'd heard them ten minutes ago. First, can you do what you are doing and glorify God? Second, can you do what you are doing and be a positive witness?

That cut me to the quick. Bridge wasn't the problem. *I was.* The next Monday morning I told my bridge partner that this was my last week. He would have to find another partner. The whole club was astonished. I have not played bridge since. I still read the bridge column in the paper almost every morning. I probably have matured enough to play the game again, but I don't have anyone to play with. When my family played cards together Joanne would sit horrified or read a magazine. We were rather competitive!

I also quit playing golf. Being a seminary student I couldn't afford the time or the money anyway. My whole life had been competitive, and I enjoyed the contest too much. God did give golf back to me four years later, but now it is just a game, an opportunity to take a walk in a park with some good friends. The score doesn't matter anymore, and the game has become a lot more enjoyable.

Something really powerful happened to me that first year in seminary. I realized that I wasn't competing with my fellow students. God had a place for every one of us, and I could genuinely pray and want the best for them as well as myself. The desire to win quietly slipped away, and was replaced by the desire to be all that God created me to be. This new desire suited my adventurous spirit, and God had an adventure in store for us.

Growing up, I was never attracted to education or books. I was too much of a free spirit, an energetic doer. When I first sensed God's calling, I was pretty sure he wanted me to be an evangelist. I would join Campus Crusade for Christ and share my faith with anyone who would listen. But something inside me began to change. When I stood up in Dallas I knew I was heading to seminary. I applied right after I got back from Dallas and was accepted in time to start that fall.

I kept a part-time position at Honeywell, since they needed me! At least that was my rationale. In truth I was keeping my foot in the door just in case I wanted to go back. Then I read in Scripture that anyone who puts his hand to the plow and looks back is not fit for the kingdom of God (Luke 9:62). So I pulled my foot out of the door after my first semester and never looked back. It was a good thing that I did, because I was tempted many times over the next few years to leave the ministry and do the simpler thing, which was being an engineer. At least I was successful at that, and I sure made a lot more money.

I loved seminary. It was the first educational experience in my life where I actually felt that way. I loved learning about God and the angels, and all the other wonderful truths about our existence. I even liked chapel. All the lifers (those who were raised in evangelical churches and made their first decision early in life) would say, "I guess we have to go to chapel." I felt like saying, "What do you mean you *have* to go. We get to go and there are a bunch of men in there singing!" For some it was "old hat," but for me everything was new and I drank it in. Christian education is more about attitude than aptitude, and such things get noticed.

One of the faculty asked if I had a position at any church. I explained that I didn't, and had been on staff with Youth for Christ, but was probably going to quit. He said, "I think I know of a church that is looking for someone like you. May I give them your phone number?" Within a day I got a call from the Minister of Adult Education at the First Baptist Church of Lakewood. The church was actually in Long Beach, California, but they never changed the name when boundary lines were redrawn. They were looking for someone to minister to their college students. I applied and they invited me to join their staff part time, beginning in June, 1973.

This new position required a move, and fortunately we were

able to sell our house. We had rented it out for a year, and the folks were now willing to buy it. So we moved into another apartment closer to the church and seminary. This was a sacrifice for Joanne, since we had owned our own home since we first married, but she took it gracefully.

I was reading an 80-year-old book entitled *Praying By the Spirit*, by R. A. Torrey. I thought it was good and decided to teach the material on Sunday mornings to the college students that summer. I advertised the chapter titles and taught one chapter a week. That is what you do when you first start your pastoral ministry. You teach dead people's notes!

Nothing was more frustrating to me than prayer. In the book were stories about people praying for hours and sometimes all night. Trying to stay focused for three minutes in prayer was an ordeal for me. My quiet times were anything but quiet. As soon as I started to pray, my mind was pummeled by all kinds of distractions. All that changed one Saturday night.

It had been a busy summer with camps and various outings with the college students. I hadn't read the last chapter in the book until the Saturday evening before I was supposed to finish the series. The title of the chapter was, "Praying by the Spirit." No reflection on R. A. Torrey, but I didn't get it. Joanne had gone to bed and I was feeling spiritually bankrupt. I was supposed to teach 150 college students the next morning and didn't have a clue what I was supposed to talk about. Such times are great moments with God! He had me right where he wanted me. I half-heartedly prayed, "Need a little help down here, Lord," and I got it.

What I learned that evening from God served as the basis for a book that I would write nearly forty years later entitled, *Liberating Prayer* (Harvest House, 2011). More importantly, it dramatically affected my relationship with God and provided an essential foundation for the kind of ministry God had in store for me (that I was yet to discover). The Lord guided me through the Scriptures that evening in a way that I have never forgotten. He showed me that effective prayer and thanksgiving were inseparable. I turned to Psalms and read, "Let us come into His presence with thanksgiving… For He is our God and we are the people of His pasture, and the sheep of his hand. Today, if you hear His voice, do not harden your hearts" (Psalm 95:2,7,8a ESV).

Until that night my prayers were simple petitions that I was bringing before God and the communication was only one way. Then the Lord brought to mind a verse from Romans, "Likewise the Spirit helps us in our weakness. For we do not know what to pray for as we ought, but the Spirit himself intercedes for us with groanings too deep for words" (Romans 8:26 ESV). In the original language the word translated as "helps" is two prepositions before the word "take." The Holy Spirit comes alongside, bears us up, and takes us across to the other side (God's presence). Any prayer that God the Holy Spirit prompts us to pray is a prayer that God the Father is always going to answer.

The truth is, I was hearing from God. It probably wasn't what I *wanted* to hear, but it was what I *needed* to hear. That is why the psalmist admonished us not to harden our hearts when we hear His voice. To better understand, think of yourself as a parent whose child is always coming to you with their requests: "Can I do this and can I have that?" Now, your child has some unresolved issues that affect your relationship with each other, and some moral issues that need to be corrected, so what is on your mind, Mom or Dad? Christianity is a relationship and God is our Father. If there are any issues between Him and us, and we let Him prioritize our prayer list, you can be assured that those issues will be at the top every time.

Knowing that God has given His children the mind of Christ (1 Corinthians 2:16), that our bodies are members of Christ (1 Corinthians 6:15), and that God has sent us the Holy Spirit who would lead us into all truth, I decided to let God speak to me. I thought, *OK God, whatever you want to talk about, I'm listening.* I spent an hour in prayer for the first time in my life. Whatever came to my mind that evening I dealt with including tempting moral issues that I had previously understood to be distractions. Those were issues God wanted me to deal with, because they were affecting my intimacy with Him. I could be totally honest with Him, because He already had perfect knowledge of me, and I was already forgiven.

I decided that evening to walk in the light and have fellowship with Him (1 John 1:7), and to live in conscious agreement about my moral condition. There would be no secrets between the two of us. I began to understand that prayer is more about listening than talking, and to be still and know that He is God. What a revelation that was! It was an essential preparation for some hard lessons yet to be learned.

4

Ministry 101

At Talbot I was elected to be a student body representative overseeing missions, and was known as the "donut man." On the way to school I would stop at a grocery store that made fresh donuts, and pick up four dozen for the student lounge. Nobody asked me to do it. It was my idea, and besides, there was nothing to munch on at the seminary. I put a cup in front of the donuts, charged ten cents, and I trusted the students to be honest. It was no big deal, but the students appreciated it. The donuts would disappear every day, and I picked up the change that covered the cost for the next day's donuts on my way home.

In December the grocery store decided to do some renovation, and the donut shop was shut down for a month. For a couple of days I received some angry words, "Hey! Where are the donuts?" So I asked them to make an announcement in chapel about the temporary stoppage, which prevented me from being tarred and feathered. No good deed goes unpunished!

As the representative for missions, I organized a trip to Urbana, Illinois over the Christmas vacation. InterVarsity Christian

Fellowship would host this missionary conference every three years, and I didn't want to miss this opportunity. Nobody had ever represented the school at this strategic event before. So I arranged for a bus to take us back. I'd been pretty successful the last time I tried such an endeavor, so why not try again? The bus was full as we started our fifty-hour journey from southern California to Illinois across the snowfields of middle America. After the first twenty-four hours on the bus the atmosphere near the back of the bus got pretty ripe, since that was the location of the toilet. Nobody wanted to give up their preferred seating up front.

I'm thankful for the experience, because I got to hear such prominent Bible teachers as Paul Little, John Stott, and many other Christian leaders. I also set up a booth and represented Talbot School of Theology. I had never considered a career in missions, but a little seed was sown in my heart that would later sprout into a global ministry.

Meanwhile, at first Baptist Church of Lakewood I reported to the Minister of Christian Education. He oversaw the children's director, youth pastor, and me. I liked him as a person, but he had a bitter dislike of the pastor, which he shared in common with the children's director and youth pastor. My heart had been poisoned toward a pastor once before, and I was not going to let it happen again. However, we met weekly and I had to endure their constant criticisms of the pastor. So I took it upon myself to establish some kind of relationship with him, with mixed results. He was a good man, but not long on relationships.

After six months the youth pastor resigned, which was good for him and the church. Meanwhile my work was bearing some fruit in the college department, although I was not aware that a small carnal group resented my attempts to deepen their walk with

God. A college ministry in a large church is quite different from a high school ministry. Many parents will require their children to go to church for a while, but there is usually a slow decline in attendance as they near their final years of high school. Nobody requires college students to go to church. They attend on their own volition.

Some are in the college department because they really want to honor God and continue on the path of sanctification. Others are there because that's where their friends are. They are a social club, a clique that excludes those who would blow the whistle on their indiscretions. One day a distraught mom and dad paid me a visit. Their daughter had been invited by the carnal group to spend a week at a beachfront property. The daughter came home a different person and was no longer interested in church. This innocent young lady had been pressured into participating in their sexual exploits, which I knew nothing about. My heart really went out to those parents. You encourage your children to go to church and that ends up being the source of their ruination. How bad is that?

I had no proof, but I did address the issue one Sunday morning without naming anyone. Carnal Christians don't like someone messing with their little club, and won't stand for it. A week later I had two co-eds come to our home on a Sunday evening to confront me. They said, "We can't trust you anymore. You share confidential information with others." I had no idea what they were talking about. I didn't want to be defensive, but I did ask, "What did I share, and with whom did I share it?" They couldn't answer directly, but enough information was given to make me aware of who leaked the information. The children's director was well known to be the church gossip, and I suspected the accuser was part of the clique.

I assured the two girls of my commitment to be trustworthy, but I could tell they were not convinced. I could have cleared my own name, but at the children's director's expense, which would have resulted in a flurry of "you said/he said" accusations. I chose to do nothing, but I did ask God, "Lord, would you let a ministry go down because of a false accusation?" I was willing to let that happen, rather than be defensive. My resolve would be tested for a year, but it proved to be a vital learning experience. Years later I would have to endure vicious slander on a national level.

The clique remained distant and stayed in their own little corner of the classroom. The majority of the group was growing and bearing fruit. A year later God exposed the source of the cancer, and it was not pretty. Those who might have been caught in the middle, quickly sided with the mature core of the class. Years later, to my regret, the children's director (who would marry the daughter of a prominent church member) was to die of AIDS.

Part of the clique was a popular guy who graduated from a university where he had been a cheerleader. No replacement was in sight for the youth pastor, so the Christian Education director decided to appoint this guy to be the interim youth pastor for the summer. I was horrified. He was not only shallower than a bird bath, I seriously questioned whether there was any water in the pool at all. I truly did not like this guy, and the Lord pressured me to ask his forgiveness for not loving him. I received a stammered response, and he quickly left. It resolved nothing between us, but it did between God and me.

I had been serving part time at the church and seriously thought about leaving after graduation from seminary. A church in Denver was looking for a Christian Education Director and they asked me to be a candidate for the position. Joanne and I drove there thinking this was an honorable way out. Everything about the position looked good. I liked the pastor, they liked me, and I liked Denver. But as we drove away, I knew I couldn't accept their offer.

Upon returning to Lakewood First Baptist I was informed that the cheerleader, who had agreed to the interim high school position, had left before he even started, to be a flight attendant for a major airline. (Four years later he too sadly died of AIDS.) The church offered me a full-time position to be the high school and college pastor, which I accepted. The previous youth pastor had bought into the notion that you should recruit the "big man" on campus, the naturally popular kid, and make him a leader in your youth group. He would attract others to come, but come to what? I had just inherited a large social club, which numbered over 200.

A Talbot student had applied to be an intern at the church. The Christian Education Director offered him an assignment to work with me. He would not have been my choice. That is a violation of Management 101. You don't hire someone to work for another person without consulting them. I just kept seeing one management faux pas after another, and that observation would weigh in heavily later in my own personal development.

My delight was the Wednesday evening Bible study for the college students. It had grown considerably the first year, and everyone looked forward to it. The clique didn't come, so we had a mature group that liked to sing, pray and learn. My cocky young intern wanted to teach that group and kept asking if he could. The high school Wednesday evening Bible study was in desperate need of help. I really hated to let it go, but I told the intern he could have the Wednesday evening college group, and I would do high school on Wednesday evenings.

Within three weeks the Wednesday night college attendance had dropped by 90 per cent, and the intern entered my office with his tail between his legs. "I suppose you want the Wednesday night Bible study back," he said. I did want it back, but that would not have been the right thing to do. I had been teaching the college students every Sunday morning and Wednesday evening, and that needed to stop. The college students didn't need another lecture. They needed to have a small group experience, where relationships could be deepened and where interactive learning could take place. I commissioned the intern to launch such a ministry. That saved face for him, and within months the numbers were back to what they had been previously.

Meanwhile, my Wednesday evenings with the high school group were a challenge. The first summer I was responsible for high school, we took 125 students to summer camp, which was the biggest number ever. Joanne came with me, and that was the end of her camping experience. A Biola student was working as a summer intern at the camp, and as Biola University required ministry students to have some Christian education assignment, I asked him if he would be interested in leading music for me on Wednesday evenings. In September we were scheduled to elect new high school student officers for the year. In the past it had been a popular election, which I was not going to repeat. We had fifteen teachers lined up to teach various electives and I met with them to share my plan.

On the first Sunday of the fall students could sign up for their choice of teachers and subjects. I thanked the last round of student leaders, introduced the teachers and asked the students to make their selection and follow their teacher to their class. After introductions were made in the class, the students were given a piece of paper, and then asked a question: "Which person in this class would you go to if you if you needed prayer or had a question about Christianity?" They were asked to write that name on the paper and hand it in. They didn't know it, but they had just elected their new student leaders. The popular kids were out of leadership and the more spiritually inclined were in. The pressure to be social was marginalized. The teachers and student leaders became the core of the high school leadership, and the whole atmosphere changed.

I asked our new youth leaders to come on Wednesday evening and not sit together, but to spread themselves out among the other students. It became their job to keep order. If any of the teachers came, they had to do the same. They could no longer sit at the back and expect me to be the master-at-arms while they watched with folded arms. Both students and teachers were asked to model the learning process by having their own Bibles open and taking notes when applicable. On the first night one of the leaders saw a student reading a secular magazine, got up, walked over to the student, took the magazine out of their hands without saying anything, and then returned to his seat. That silent act spoke volumes.

The biggest mistake churches make concerning discipline is to expect the master of ceremonies to also be the master-at-arms. Peer discipline works the best. If a student whispered or was disruptive, it was the responsibility of the student leader or teacher closest to the person to do something. Within a month we had 100 students singing and quietly learning together.

Although I felt the youth ministry was on the right track, I knew I was I not called to be a youth pastor. I told the pastor he needed to start looking for someone else, and I would help with the search even if it meant my leaving the church, or returning to a part-time position. He was disappointed but understood. Meanwhile I was having a new problem with the college department. Some had married each other and didn't want to leave the group. So I started the Merry Mates, a class for young married couples, and asked them to come to that class instead of attending the college group. It worked, and the class grew to about fifty couples.

The Christian Education director suffered an accident at home that left him somewhat impaired and on crutches. To my relief, during his convalescence, he accepted an offer to go elsewhere. The church asked me to take over his duties and I became the Minister of Adult Education. We need to hire a new youth pastor and my humbled young college intern took over that ministry. The children's director had to report to me, and he heard in no uncertain terms that his wagging tongue would have to stop, or he would lose it.

Years later I would tell my seminary students that loyalty to their senior pastor was not an option. If they could not in good conscience support the person they were reporting to, they had no choice but to leave. I promised them that their loyalty would be tested. Church members and other staff would come to them and ask what they think of the pastor or his messages. They should answer, "You are talking to the wrong person. If you have a problem with the pastor, you need to talk to him." Loyalty does not mean silence, and everyone should give honest feedback to the person they report to – if it is done constructively. The enemy will sow seeds of disunity in every Christian ministry. I could not help but smile when I overheard one member say to another, "It wouldn't do any good to see Neil, he would just tell you to go see the pastor." Message received!

We were a church with over 2,000 members, and our weakest ministry was visitation. The responsibility had fallen by default on a dear old retired pastor who worked part time with the seniors. He would plead for volunteers to come out on the first Monday evening of the month to call upon visitors. About twenty would come, half of whom you hoped wouldn't! Visitor cards were distributed and off they went – to do what? I had no idea and I don't think they did either.

Evangelism was my first love when I sensed the call to ministry, but that had all but disappeared. I was stuck in the holy huddle. All my friends were Christians and I had lost touch with the world. I would give my obligatory challenge to be good witnesses and everyone would go home scared and feeling guilty. I clearly remember to this day when I became aware of my own lack of interest in reaching the lost and for the church's lack of ministry to the hurting humanity that was all around us. So I prayed, "Lord, let me see the world the way you see it, and change my heart to be like yours." Any time you sincerely pray like that, be prepared for something to happen.

I shared my concern with the pastor and volunteered to set up a training program based on Evangelism Explosion, founded by Dr. James Kennedy. He gladly accepted my idea and commissioned me to start that fall. There was a problem, he didn't notify the retired pastor who held all the first-time attender cards. Just another administrative goof that created a tension between me and the retired pastor. So I apologized to this dear man and asked if he would talk to the pastor with me. It wasn't necessary, he gladly deferred when I explained my plan.

The genius of the program was on-the-job training. New students would go with a trained person as they called on visitors to the church. The problem was we didn't have any trained person to lead. So that fall I trained myself. I personally called on everyone who visited our church for the first time, which then wasn't a huge number. As I drove to make my first visit I went with the determination to find out if they were Christians and not to leave until I'd shared the gospel with them if they weren't. I would use the two Evangelism Explosion questions which were:

1. If you died tonight, do you know where you would spend eternity?

2. If God asked you on what basis you had a right to be there, how would you answer?

With all my fumbling around it took me almost an hour to find out that they were believers. I continue visiting all fall until I felt that I was ready to train some others, and then I prayerfully invited twenty mature adult believers to meet with me one night. I shared my plan and asked them to make a commitment to stay with me for a year. I said that I would train them first, and then we would select twenty others to join us. I was hoping that four would make such a commitment. I was surprised when eighteen said they would. The other couple wanted to as well, but they couldn't, because of the night we chose to meet.

So I taught and we role-played for a few weeks. Then I gave them a simple survey that we would take door to door in our community on a Saturday morning. The purpose was to help them get over the fear factor. I had tried the survey myself at Long Beach State University. I would stop a student and ask, "Would you be willing to answer a couple questions?" One young man agreed, so I asked him. "According to your understanding, who is Jesus Christ?" "A figment of your imagination," he said. Then I asked, "According to your understanding, how does one become a Christian?" He answered, "Applied stupidity." This was not ripe fruit!

I said, "Something must have turned you off Christianity, and

I would be interested to know what that was." He was interested in telling me, and I listened for half an hour. I told him, "If that had been my experience I would be turned off as well. However, I've had just the opposite experience, and if anyone should ask you how to become a real Christian, you can give them this tract." He took the tract I proffered, thanked me, and left.

That Saturday morning, my faithful students led two people to Christ. The next week we divided nine visitor cards between us and they made their first calls. We never had a week go by when there wasn't at least one decision for Christ. When they felt they were ready to train others, I asked them for names they would like to recommend for the next group of trainees. Two of the original group said they wanted to go through the training one more time before they took on someone else, now we had seventeen couples making visits every week. I personally invited sixteen others – all recommended by the first group – to join us and challenged them to stay with the program for nine months. They accepted. Jesus never asked for volunteers. He prayerfully selected his disciples. If everybody is qualified, then quality people don't sign up. A ministry like this must start with mature Christians. You can't make a strong chain with weak links.

In the beginning we met one night a week at 7:00 p.m.. I would teach for half an hour, and then send them out. There would be another half hour of discussion when they returned. The class was set up for sixteen weeks. During that time the trainees would read a book, and the trainers would read a second book. Around the tenth week the trainees were to take the initiative when they called upon the visitors. A strange thing happened when we took on new recruits. The number of visitors doubled. Every new convert has approximately ten people they connect with socially. If we win one of them to Christ, they have ten new contacts in our community. When churches don't reach out they become insular and cease being the salt and light that every community needs.

When our numbers doubled again, so did the visitors. A year later we had 100 people going out weekly on three different nights. That year we took on 300 new members and most were new converts.

One day my secretary came into my room and closed the door behind her. "I can't keep going this way," she said. She was a lovely person, but I had no idea what she was talking about. I discovered that I was a stress carrier. I wasn't stressing out, but everyone around me was. Dad had taught me how to work, but I couldn't blame him that I'd become a workaholic. Joanne was also distraught that I was gone almost every night of the week. Something had to change.

Meanwhile, I was being challenged with another reality. A female Bible teacher in our church referred a young lady to me. Looking like the classic flower child of the sixties, this 26-year-old walked in my office with a tear-stained Bible. She had graduated from college, but had wandered the streets ever since. We talked for a couple of hours and she couldn't give me a good timeline of the last five years. She had been diagnosed a paranoid schizophrenic, and had been hospitalized three different times.

This was way over my head, but I told her I would be willing to meet with her again if she came under the authority of the church. I don't really know why I said that to her, but as soon as I did, she jumped out of her chair and said in a different voice, "I have to get out of here," and walked out the door. I followed her and asked if Jesus was her Lord. At the bottom of the stairs, she turned around and said, "Yes." Then I asked, "Can we go back to my room and talk?" Again she said, "Yes," and we walked back up the stairs to my office. I went for some help, but there was no one around.

I said, "There is a spiritual battle going on in your mind. Has anyone ever talked to you about this before?" She said, "No, they were either afraid, or didn't know." But she knew. That was my first encounter with someone who clearly had a demonic problem. In my naiveté I assumed she must have been dabbling in the occult or involved in some gross immorality. Neither one was the case. So what do you do? I certainly didn't know what to do. My seminary education had never touched on the subject.

I was able to ascertain that the symptoms started after her well-known pediatrician father had run off with his nurse and left the family. Most of the family had vented their rage, but she did the "Christian" thing and lied to herself emotionally. The anger was there, but she buried it. Over the next few weeks, two verses came to my attention in a new way that I had never seen before:

> *Therefore, having put away falsehood, let each one of you speak the truth with his neighbor, for we are members one of another. Be angry and do not sin; do not let the sun go down on your anger, and give no opportunity to the devil.*
>
> Ephesians 4:25–26 ESV

> *... [casting] all your anxieties on Him, because He cares for you. Be sober-minded; be watchful. Your adversary the devil prowls around like a roaring lion, seeking someone to devour.*
>
> 1 Peter 5:7–8 ESV

Having taken a course on hermeneutics I knew that nothing has meaning without context, and to understand certain verses one should go back and look at the previous verses. The subjects before the warnings about Satan were anger and anxiety. Anger and anxiety are just human emotions, but they are often preceded by ungodly thoughts and beliefs. I believe that we can draw some important conclusions from these passages. If we can't speak the truth in love and learn how to properly manage our emotional life we may be spiritually vulnerable to Satan's attacks.

It would be years before I learned that what the young woman really needed to do was forgive her father. However, I was able to provide her with some help. Initially, I couldn't even mention her father without her threatening to leave the room. Months later she had put on twenty much-needed pounds in weight and shared a testimony before 400 teenagers that left us all in tears.

One other experience aroused my curiosity. A man in his twenties with some obvious problems would wander around outside our church. One day I got a call from the secretaries who were having lunch in a large classroom that doubled as our lunch room. This man had entered the room uninvited and was writing little words on a chalkboard and then erasing them. The secretaries called me for help. I asked him if we could go outside and talk, which we did. He worked in a nearby car wash, and I just assumed he had some history with drugs. I invited him to attend church that Sunday, and he left.

Three weeks later I was in my office preparing for that night's service, when my phone rang. This young man was downstairs and wanted to see me. I invited him in for a chat, but I was pressed for time. So I simply asked him if he had ever made a decision for Christ. Instantly I sensed incredible spiritual opposition, and he was struck by fear. He couldn't respond to me, so I said, "There is a spiritual battle for your mind, I'm going to pray, and when you're able, just call upon the Lord Jesus to save you." I prayed out loud for several minutes. Finally he spoke, with what seemed like a tremendous struggle: one word was slowly followed by another: "Lord… Jesus… I need you!" Instantly the oppression left and he looked up at me with tears in his eyes and said, "I'm free!"

This left-brained engineer had a lot to learn. These experiences did not take a lot of discernment, but they raised a lot of questions in my mind. Were they an anomaly, and how many others struggled with the enemy? If we wrestle not with flesh and blood, then the primary battle is spiritual. This has profound implications for how we understand mental health and how to be more effective in evangelism. The answers were slow in coming.

I thank God for those three and half years at Lakewood First Baptist. It was a crash course in Ministry 101, and I learned a lot of valuable lessons. I could have easily fallen into a maintenance pattern and continued with what I was doing for the rest of my life. Little did I know at the time that my life and ministry would go much deeper and wider. It was with a tearful goodbye that I left to be the pastor at Pacific View Baptist Church in Torrance, California.

5

Struck Down

Not only was my time at Lakewood First Baptist a crash course in ministry, but that was the church where I was ordained by the Baptist General Conference, pioneered by Swedish Baptist immigrants. Their primary center of location was Minnesota, but I had never heard of the denomination when I lived there. It seemed almost providential that I would connect with them in California. In three and a half years I had progressed from a part-time college pastor, to a full-time youth and college pastor, to a minister of adult education. I had started a ministry of evangelism that was bearing a lot of fruit. The church hired three new staff after I left, partly due to recent growth. So why did I leave?

When I first sensed a call to ministry, I knew very little about myself, and even less about God. I had no idea what my gifts were or what my potential was. I really had no vision other than being the pastor of a small country church like the one I grew up in. In those three plus years I started to realize that my gifts were more suited to preaching and teaching. So I started taking part-time classes at Talbot to finish my Master of Divinity Degree. The call to be a senior pastor was irresistible, but I was not anticipating the trial that awaited me.

Pacific View Baptist Church was a mission church in Torrance, California. Three men had left an American Baptist Church to plant a General Conference church. They called their first pastor, who served six years, and then went back to the motherland (Minnesota) to be a district superintendent. The church had no facilities, and was meeting in a Seventh-day Adventist Church, which permitted us to use their building on Sunday. Two years had passed since the first senior pastor left. The youth pastor had been taking care of the pastoral duties while guest speakers filled the pulpit.

I had accepted the call on the condition that they would be willing to change their bylaws, which specified four boards! The four boards met once a month, and I had to choose which board to meet with the first month I was there. Flushed with my recent evangelism experiences I chose to meet with the "Board of World Evangelization," which consisted of four people. With such a lofty title, one would hope for something significant. Unfortunately their vision had not progressed beyond writing some letters and disbursing a few dollars to those laboring in other countries. One member was a lady who was married to her third husband, who was a Mormon. She was in charge of small group Bible studies, which were non-existent at the time. Another member was a dear old saint, who was truly a good man in his eighties, but deaf. The chairwoman was a sweet person who had never considered the need for diet and exercise. The fourth man held some promise. When I shared my plans for visitation evangelism, they asked how they could help. I said, "I'll get back with you." I went home that night a little disheartened. Dedicated incompetency is still incompetency, which is probably what led someone to observe that "a camel was a horse designed by a church committee."

The four boards reported to an advisory committee, which had no authority other than to advise, but they were the unofficial leaders of the church. I began working with them to rewrite the by-laws that would enable us to have one official board of elders. Within six months we had amended the by-laws and the church constitution, which were ratified by the congregation. Then I made one of the biggest mistakes of my life. The church voted in five elders who were all given a five-year term. We should have staggered their commitment.

Most churches have learned to appoint deacons and elders with staggered three-year terms. That way the board is renewed every year. Suppose an unqualified person is chosen to be on the board, or an appointed member starts having personal or interpersonal struggles, what then? With staggered terms, if no one has the courage to confront the situation, they will eventually leave the board when their term is up and little damage is done.

I was stuck with five men for five years, if I stayed that long. They were all charter members, and I found out after I left the church that they would have a secret birthday party every year to which only charter members were invited. After all, it was their church! The daughter of one of the elders came home from college, saw the new growth in the church and was overheard saying, "Who are all these new people? They shouldn't be new members of *our* church unless they are approved by the charter members."

We did experience a lot of growth initially, and, like any honeymoon, it came to an abrupt end. A power struggle was developing on the board, centring around one man. Ironically he was the one most emphatic about inviting me as a candidate.

At board meetings he would make comments like: "People are saying…" Of course, I couldn't leave that unchallenged so I asked, "Who's saying that?" "Well, I would rather not say," he answered. "Then I would rather not hear," I responded, "because it makes all the difference in the world who is saying it." The board knew he was the only one saying these things, and he withdrew the statements.

I always saw myself as a peacemaker, and I certainly didn't want to fight my own board. On the other hand, I was not easily intimidated, nor was I afraid of confrontation. So I called him to ask if I could stop by his home. At the time I had my own 48-hour rule. If I sensed that something was wrong between myself and anyone else I would not let 48 hours go by without seeing that person. The idea was not to confront them, but to find out if I had done something negative that had affected our relationship.

At his home I told him that I didn't feel good about our relationship and asked if I had done anything to offend him. He assured me that I hadn't. However, I knew nothing had been resolved, so I asked if he would meet with me once a week to share any concerns that he had with me and with my ministry. I encouraged him to be totally honest with me in private rather than sharing such concerns at board meetings.

We met weekly on Monday mornings for breakfast. I hated those weekly meetings. Every morning was a sparring match and it went on for six months. I can honestly say that I had no motive to change or correct him. I only wanted to establish some kind of a meaningful relationship. It was not to be. I thought I could get along with anyone, but I learned the hard way that you can't be reconciled with another person if they don't want to be. The Bible teaches: "If possible, so far as it depends on you, live peaceably with all" (Romans 12:18 ESV). But it doesn't always depend on us.

In the middle of that six-month ordeal I requested permission from the church board to put together a tour to Israel and offered to use my vacation time. But my nemesis was against it, and said, "I know how these things work, if he can get enough people to go with him, he can go free, and that is like giving him a bonus." Not wanting to create any more tension on the board, I withdrew my request and used my vacation time to go with another group. It turned out to be one of the greatest spiritual blessings of my life. If nothing else it ended those dreaded Monday morning breakfasts!

As the tour guide led us through the Church of All Nations in the Garden of Gethsemane, I knew why I was there. This beautiful structure situated outside the Eastern Gate of the old walled city of Jerusalem at the base of the Mount of Olives enshrines the rock where it is believed that Jesus prayed, "Father, if You are willing, remove this cup from Me; yet not My will, but Yours be done" (Luke 22:42). The next day I returned to that holy place by myself. I silently sat for most of the afternoon knowing in my heart that I was in the right place at a very special time of my life. This location is where Jesus fought His lonely battle. The mockery of a trial and the death march to the cross were yet ahead, but the crisis of the will had come to resolution, for which we are all eternally grateful.

In the throes of extreme agony Jesus voluntarily chose to take the sins of the whole world upon Himself. This divine moment went way beyond textbook learning in my inner being: I sensed a renewing in my spirit to the purpose of the cross and the message of forgiveness. I was rejoicing in the cleansing of my own spirit. I also understood in a way I had never known before that I needed to forgive as I had been forgiven. Jesus had to take all the sins of the world on Himself and all God was asking me to do was to take the sin of one man upon myself. I could do that. I *would* do that.

I returned home a different person and the atmosphere at our next board meeting seemed to improve. Not having me to pick on anymore, he went after my youth pastor. That did it! I don't know about you, but I can take a lot more criticism than I can watch innocent people take. During the December board meeting I took my stand. I told the board that they had to do something about my nemesis or I was resigning. As far as I was concerned our relationship was a sham, a disgrace to Christianity, and I wasn't going to have any part of it. In hindsight it was really bad timing to force the issue right before Christmas.

The board met without us and three weeks later I received a letter. "We have arranged a meeting for the two of you to ask each other for forgiveness and then we can continue with our building plans." I was so disappointed. *Great,* I thought, *sweep it under the carpet and we can trip over it later!* I did go to the meeting and I did ask him to forgive me for not loving him, because I didn't, and I did not feel good about that. This was the third time I had to ask someone I detested to forgive me for lack of love. But I did not back down from my earlier stand. The rest of the board agreed with me in private, but not necessarily in public. Since the board had not dealt with the real issue, I decided to follow through on my commitment and resign.

Shortly thereafter I got the flu. It wasn't the horrendous kind, but I felt like I shouldn't subject the church to my illness. Our denominational leader spoke in my place and then joined my family for dinner at our home. He was really pleased by the progress in our church. We had doubled in size and had plans to build new facilities at a new location that God had given to us. Then I told him of my plans to resign. He was shocked and disagreed with my decision, but my mind was made up. I couldn't be shaken from my convictions if I knew I was right, but I could also be stubborn when my fallen nature thought I was right. I was about to learn the difference.

I stayed home for two days to make sure I was over the flu and on Wednesday morning I wrote out my resignation. By Wednesday evening my temperature was 103.5 degrees, and I'd totally lost my voice. I have never been so sick before or since. It doesn't take a genius to recognize that God was not pleased with my decision. I did not resign that next Sunday, not because I was too sick, but because I still didn't have a voice to speak.

When you are flat on your back there is nowhere to look but up. I was reading through the Gospel of Mark when I came to the following passage (8:22–25 NASB):

> *And they came to Bethsaida. And they brought a blind man to Jesus and implored Him to touch him. Taking the blind man by the hand, He brought him out of the village; and after spitting on his eyes and laying His hands on him, He asked him, "Do you see anything?" And he looked up and said, "I see men, for I see them like trees, walking around." Then again He laid His hands on his eyes; and he looked intently and was restored, and began to see everything clearly.*

I got the message. I was seeing him like a tree. He was an obstacle in my path. He was blocking my goal. Oh no he wasn't. I was! In truth, God used that man more than any other man on this planet to make me the pastor that God wanted me to be. We make plans and think we know how we are going to get there. Then God comes along and plops a tree right in our path and says, "There, what are you going to do about that?" The flesh is quick to answer,

"Get me a chain saw!"

I confessed, "Lord, I don't love that man, but I know You do. There is nothing within me to love him except for You, so You are going to have to touch me." God did touch me! God loved this man, because God is love. It is His nature to love us, and He wants that to be our nature as well. The love of God is not dependent upon the object of love. That is why God's love is unconditional.

After two weeks of recovery I was finally able to preach again. With a husky voice, I spoke on that passage in Mark. I told the congregation that there are three types of people in this world. First, there are those who are blind. Satan has blinded the minds of the unbelieving (2 Corinthians 4:4). They need you and me to take their hands and lead them to Jesus.

Second, there are those who see people like trees. We compare our leaves with one another and scratch each other with our branches. But we are not trees. We are children of God, who are created in His image.

Third, there are people who see clearly; they have been touched by God. I confessed to them my own independence and pledged my love to them. I gave an invitation that morning and I don't even remember what for. I was not prepared for what happened next.

People all over the auditorium came forward. There wasn't room in the front of the church to accommodate them so the doors were opened up and the people spilled out onto the lawn. The organist and pianist couldn't keep playing because of the tears rolling down their cheeks. People were reaching across the aisles, asking each other to forgive them. I hadn't even talked about that! There were no more than fifteen people still seated. Would you care to guess the identity of one of them! To my knowledge, the man never did change. Maybe he didn't need to, but I did. I was never the same again. Nobody can explain what happened that morning apart from the grace of God. It was a mighty movement of His Spirit when this pastor got his own heart right with God.

I started to understand that it was my job to catch the fish. It was God's job to clean them. He is the One who will convict the world of sin, not me. I never had to ask anyone after that to forgive me for not loving them. Years later I told my seminary students that story and said, "If you are called to be a pastor, there is one criterion for success that is not negotiable. The bottom line is, you have to love people. If people know that you love them, you can make a lot of mistakes. However, if they question your love, all it takes is one mistake and you will be on the hot seat." Jesus said, "By this all people will know that you are my disciples, if you have love for one another" (John 13:35 ESV).

My personal goal was to be like Jesus and be known for my love, but that is a lifetime process. My ministry goal was to glorify God by bearing much fruit. To accomplish that I had to learn how to abide in Christ and be led by His Holy Spirit, for apart from Christ we can do nothing (John 15:5). If everything we accomplish in our lives could be explained by hard work or human ingenuity, then where was God and who gets the glory? I learned to declare my dependency upon God and ask him to fill me with His Holy Spirit before I started any ministry.

We started a second service each Sunday morning to accommodate our growth in numbers, but we were stuck in rented property and going nowhere. However, I began to sense that God was going to do something in our church that year. I even shared my impressions with the congregation. One Sunday morning I said, "Something is going to happen this year that we cannot take credit for." Shortly thereafter my secretary informed me that a realtor wanted to see me. He was representing a construction firm that was looking for available space to build houses. He had tracked us down to see if we would be willing to sell our property. Before I had arrived at the church, the previous leaders had pieced together some property, but it didn't hold much promise for being a good church site. The contractor wanted the property to build some houses.

Given the difficulty of finding available property in this coastal community, I informed him that we wouldn't be interested in selling. He asked if we especially wanted that property, or if we would be willing to build somewhere else. I felt a little uncomfortable speaking for the church, but I didn't like the property or its location. We chatted for awhile and he left with the impression that we would be willing to sell the property if he could find something else better for us.

A week later he wanted to show me a piece of property that he thought would be much better for the church. To my surprise he showed me five vacant acres situated perfectly in the centre of our community. He thought the price would be reasonable since it had been tied up in litigation. A bank had repossessed the property and had been holding it for ten years while paying the taxes. I asked him to give us a bid for our old property. It was time to inform the board.

The board was as pleased and surprised as I was that such property was still available. The church met and we all agreed to offer a bid for the property, not to exceed $500,000. This was a middle- to upper-middle-class coastal community in 1978, so we all had our doubts that we could actually purchase a property of that size for such a low price. We started negotiations with the bank by making an offer of $400,000. We were all pleasantly surprised to receive an offer of $325,000 for our old property. For $75,000 we could double our acreage and move to a much better location.

On a Friday morning I heard from the bank that they had turned us down. I drove to the bank to retrieve our bid, and asked if the person responsible for the property was there. He was and he invited me into his office. I felt led to say, "We are just a nickel and dime operation, and I am authorized to counter-offer $425,000. Are we wasting our time?" He informed me that three vice-presidents, of which he was one, had to agree on such a sale, and one of the other two was present. He excused himself to talk with the other vice-president. Less than five minutes later he came back with a signed and amended contract for $425,000. I was elated and so was the church. For $100,000 we were getting what we'd thought weeks earlier would be unimaginable.

While waiting for the contracts to close, we put together a building committee, and started making plans for this "gift from God." Days before we were supposed to close on our old property, the realtor paid me another visit with some very bad news. The contractor he represented was backing out of the deal. "Can he do that?" I asked. The realtor thought he legally could, and shared how sorry he was. "I have represented him for twenty-five years and he has never done that before. I think he is having some family problems. His daughter has multiple sclerosis and is living with them since her husband left her."

I shared the bad news that Sunday morning with the board, and they were upset. Some wanted to take legal action against the contractor. I was deeply disappointed in them, and said I would have no part in any such litigation. Our ministry was to help hurting people, not sue them! The next Tuesday I was holding my regular visitation evangelism class and I sensed the Lord leading me to visit the contractor, whom I had never met. To my surprise, his phone number and address were listed in the phone book.

I drove up to his listed address doubting that I would have any chance to see him in this upscale community, since most of the homes were behind gates. To my surprise his home wasn't! The house was huge; I wasn't sure where the front door was. As I was walking by the kitchen window their maid saw me and asked through the open window what I was doing there. I said I was there to see the contractor. He wasn't home, but his wife and daughter were home and she invited me in. In their large master bedroom, I met his wife and daughter, whose physical impairment was obvious.

I introduced myself and said, "I have never met your husband, but we had a business deal that fell through. I sensed that he was a hurting person, and I wanted to come by to see if I could do anything to help." I found out that the mother and daughter were attending a religious cult, but I also noticed that they were reading Chuck Colson's book, *Born Again*. An hour later I had the privilege to lead both of them to Christ.

I fairly flew off that mountain of affluence in my pastoral limousine, which was a VW Bug. The next day the realtor called, and said, "I don't know what you did yesterday, but the deal is back on. But he has lowered his offer to $300,000." We gladly accepted that offer, because it was still a very good deal.

It was a test. God wanted to give us that property, but He wanted to know what we would do with it. There were 8,000 people who lived within a four-block radius of that location, and He wanted us to be a beacon of light for the lost.

Shortly thereafter I had lunch with another realtor who was

also the mayor of the city. I asked him about the possibility of getting a builder's permit for a church on the new location. He shared that our parcel was one of four such plots that had been in litigation for about ten years. A large contracting firm had wanted to build low-income housing, and the city had quickly re-zoned to stop that from happening. So this prime property had sat vacant for ten years with neither side moving. He advised us to sell the property, because he had serious doubts about us ever being given permission by the city to build. That could be a lethal blow, since the mayor knew the real estate market and the politics of that community.

About the same time I received another caller at our church office. This man was a lawyer who represented the larger construction firm. They were about to make a deal with the city to stop the litigation if they would let them build upscale condominiums. They owned the other three plots, and wanted to buy ours, which I informed them was not for sale. They offered us $750,000, and I was beginning to wonder if I was in the wrong business!

The construction company proceeded to make plans and presentations to the planning committee and we attended with great interest. There were some serious zoning questions that affected how residential housing interfaced with commercial businesses in the area. During one meeting, a council member pointed out that it would be a lot easier if we would exchange our five acres with one of the five-acre plots the construction company owned. The lawyer came to us with an offer. They would exchange their five acres for ours, clear the property of all debris, give us fill-dirt for a low spot and $200,000 cash. We agreed, especially since our architect said the new property was much better located.

Now we were starting our building program with the property

debt free, the ground cleared (which took two end-dump trucks a week of hauling), and $75,000 cash in our pockets. Halfway through construction, our contractor said that he'd been playing golf the previous weekend and an old friend asked him what he was doing. He said, "I'm building a church building" and shared with him the location. His friend said, "You are not going to believe this. Their pastor struck a deal for that property for $425,000 a couple years back and that very afternoon I submitted a $600,000 bid for the same property."

I believe God wants to build His church, but he has to lay the right foundation in us first, because *we* are the church. The apostle Peter wrote, "For it is time for judgment to begin at the household of God; and if it begins with us, what will be the outcome for those who do not obey the gospel of God" (1 Peter 4:17). The process of building first begins in the life of the pastor. People cannot rise above their leadership. I thank God to this day for striking me down. If my stubbornness had won the day, I would have resigned and that would have been the end of my pastoral journey, just another pastor who started a couple of bonfires and flamed out.

6

God's Ministry of Darkness

Before our church relocated to our new land and facilities, I was teaching on the kingdom of God at Wednesday night Bible studies. I had put together a syllabus that was way too advanced for most believers. It must have been incredibly boring, but some attended anyway.

Studying the kingdom theme of Scripture was personally enlightening, but it also raised a curious question. Why hadn't I been taught about the other kingdom, the kingdom of darkness? Scripture clearly reveals both kingdoms. As believers we have been delivered out of the kingdom of darkness and transferred into the kingdom of God's beloved Son (Colossians 1:13). Both kingdoms are operating simultaneously in this present world, and in our churches as well.

The church was in the process of raising funds for our new building, hiring a contractor, and breaking ground on the new property. While preparing for a message on stewardship I was reading the prophet Haggai, and I came across the following words (Haggai 1:2–4 ESV):

> *"Thus says the Lord of hosts: These people say the time has not yet come to rebuild the house of the Lord." Then the word of the Lord came by the hand of Haggai the prophet, "Is it a time for you yourselves to dwell in your paneled houses, while this house lies in ruins?"*

Later in the passage it instructs them to go up to the hills and bring wood and build the house (1:8). The problem for me was, all my elders lived in paneled homes in nearby hills (including my nemesis who could have funded the entire building program without altering his lifestyle!) I couldn't use that passage, because the application was too obvious, or could I? I shared my concern with Joanne on our daily walk, and by the time we finished I knew what I had to do.

So the next Sunday I chose to let the Word speak for itself. I wasn't trying to produce guilt in anyone, and I made sure the congregation knew that. Before the service started I noticed that two new families were in attendance with five teenage children. These are the kind of visitors that churches like ours really desire. My first thought was, *Why this Sunday?* I didn't like giving messages on stewardship anyway, but liked it even less when I saw them.

Halfway through my message, a young man seated in the overflow area suddenly fell from his chair with what appeared to be a seizure. Two doctors were summoned from the congregation, but I sensed that something else was going on. It was totally out of character for me, but I prayed out loud, "In the name of the Lord Jesus Christ, I command Satan to release [the young man]." I even surprised myself. I found out after the service that the "seizure" stopped immediately and the doctors could find no further problem. The young man was anything but a spiritual giant, and was obviously vulnerable to such attacks.

After the service our board chairman said, "I didn't like the way you prayed. It implied that he had a spiritual problem." I said, "I didn't imply anything. I sensed that it was a spiritual problem, and it was. Go and ask those attending him what happened right after I prayed." He never got back to me. That week I was doing my visitation evangelism, and was anxiously looking forward to calling on the two families who'd visited that Sunday. Both families were at the first home I called on. I didn't know if they would be turned on or turned off. They were friends looking to join another church and were discussing my message when I came. To my surprise they enthusiastically said, "We're coming to your church."

One Sunday a man talked to me after church and said, "Pastor, I have this voice in my head!" Not only did I not know what that was, I wouldn't have had any idea how to deal with it. Consequently, he continued to struggle and be a negative influence at home and in the church. If that happened today, I would have said, "Let's get together this week. I can help you get rid of that." This is painful to recall, because he really needed the church to help him, and I couldn't.

A lady had joined our church with seven foster children, who came from three different families. When her husband died, she adopted all seven. Two biological sisters had unique problems. One appeared to be mentally disabled. Every time someone prayed in the church, she would get up and leave. I went with the mother on an appointment with the school counselor to talk about the sister with mental disabilities. Her characteristics were not like those of most children with similar problems, which raised my suspicions, but I had no idea what to do about it.

The other sister was the surprise. She was a very quiet and

frail young lady. We found out she was having sex at home with one of the adopted brothers. That young boy had confessed it to the youth pastor, and the youth pastor had called both of them in to talk while I informed the mother. Our plan was to bring the three together. The boy had run away before, and we were trying to prevent that from happening again. The boy was obviously remorseful and we excused him. The mother couldn't handle it, and left before we could even bring them together. The girl's response was totally unexpected. She glared at me and said, "You stupid–" I dismissed the boy and asked my secretary to join me with the girl. Neither of us had any question as to what we were dealing with. The presence of evil would have been obvious to anyone. We worked for three hours and she finally made some profession of faith. Unfortunately, her mother dismissed the whole affair. Such experiences left me with a lot of questions, and subsequent answers would shape my future ministry.

Three years into this pastorate, Joanne started to develop cataracts in both eyes. In those days they would not do lens implants. They could not guarantee the longevity of the implants unless you were over sixty. Today, it would be a simple day surgery. Both her eyes clouded up, and I excused her from any ministry duties and responsibilities. Being a pastor's wife is difficult enough, and facing eye surgery was overwhelming. I knew I had to do something to get her out of the role of being a pastor's wife, which she never cared for anyway. Joanne is a private person and does not relish the spotlight. I couldn't leave, however, until the church buildings were complete. She had to come first, before the ministry.

Finding an alternative way to minister was my motivation to get my doctorate. I had no idea what God would do with that, but I wanted to be prepared for whatever it was. So I started working on my doctorate at Pepperdine University. The degree was in Institutional Management in the School of Education and Psychology. Classes were geared toward the working professional. Most of the students were teachers, and principals in public education. I chose this direction because seminary had offered me nothing on leadership and management. I had experienced my share of managerial goofs in the midst of organizational pathology.

It was a refreshing experience. I had been in full-time ministry for eight years and this afforded me the experience of interacting with the world again. One class was on Change Theory. The professor started the class by having us complete some statements like "Change is…" and "When I see change coming I…"

I was surprised to find out that I was the only one in the class who saw change as good and would be excited about it. All the others were highly educated people, but had a negative reaction to change. I asked the professor about it, and he said, "You represent less than 5 per cent of the population. People are generally more comfortable with the status quo, and will naturally resist change." That knowledge of myself and of the way the majority thought was invaluable to me.

I wrote a paper about my church experience of changing the by-laws which the elders had previously put together; of selling the land which the elders had purchased; and of changing the style of ministry which the elders had instituted. The professor, an ex-Jesuit priest, asked me, "How did you survive?" I was wondering that myself. Everyone at church would agree that the new by-laws, land, and ministry were an improvement, but why did I have bullet holes all over me?

Another class was on Forecasting, which taught us how to make predictions for the future and how it would affect our organizations. All the students had to make presentations. An inner city principal's presentation was about astral projection, channeling spirits, reading minds, and so on. It piqued the interest of the other students. The lure of knowledge and power is universal and timeless. I waited until the end of class to ask, "When you were researching this, did you ask yourself the question, is this right or wrong?" "I'm not interested in that," he said. To which I responded, "I would be if I were you. Everything you described is as old as biblical history and God explicitly forbids it."

It was late and the professor called it a night. Now I was surrounded by most of the students, who wanted to know what is wrong with what the principal had shared. I told them it was nothing but the occult. Actually, he was being deceived ahead of the times. He was describing the New Age movement that was just starting to take root in our country.

Meanwhile, back at the church we were preparing for an open house with our newly completed facilities. We had planned for some time to invite the community to come by on a Sunday afternoon and walk through the church buildings. The week before we'd asked for volunteers to come to the church on Saturday morning before the open house and help distribute invitations to our immediate community. Not one of my elders showed up. None of them would join me with visitation evangelism either.

I was relieved when I sensed that God had released me from that pastorate. A lot was accomplished. On paper it would appear to have been a successful ministry, but for me it was pastoral boot camp. I left a better person, and that made it worth the trip. Three months after we dedicated the new buildings I resigned to finish my doctorate. I heard later that the board asked the church leaders to extend their time in office as elders to ensure continuity during the transition between pastors, but they were all voted out.

I took a year off for study, and study I did. That year I completed forty-three semester units, finished the Master of Divinity degree, the course work for the Doctor of Education degree, took my comprehensive exams, did my research, and wrote my dissertation. When you take a year off for study with no income, you squeeze in as much as you can.

We started that year with the assurance of a friend that $20,000 dollars would be made available interest free in two $10,000 instalments. The plan was to pay off the loan when we sold our home. Not having to sell our house allowed us to keep our children in the same school for that year. After I completed my education, I was confident that God would have a place for us. So I proceeded with finishing my doctorate and a second master's degree with a great deal of anticipation. For the next six months our life unfolded as planned, then God turned out the lights.

The second half of the promised $20,000 wasn't going to be available! Having no other source of income our cupboards went bare. I had no job and my educational goals were only half completed. I always considered myself a faithful person, but now I was on the brink of not being able to provide for the basic needs of my family. I had been so certain of God's calling six months earlier, but the darkness of uncertainty had settled in.

It all culminated two weeks before my comprehensive exams. Only 10 per cent of the doctoral candidates had passed the previous comprehensive exams, which took place on two consecutive Saturdays and were offered only three times a year. I was sensing a lot of pressure. If I didn't pass the exams, I couldn't start my research and dissertation. I had already invested three years of my life and $15,000 dollars in the program. Now I didn't even know where my next meal was coming from. I had equity in my home, but the year was 1980 and interest rates at the time were so high that houses weren't selling. The tension to create my own light was overwhelming. I looked into a couple of ministry opportunities, but I knew they weren't right for me, and I couldn't accept them. The problem wasn't an unwillingness to work, I would have sold hotdogs to provide for my family. I wasn't struggling with pride, at least not this time; I just wanted to know God's will!

I began to wonder if I had made the wrong decision. His leading had been so clear the past summer. Why was I walking in darkness? It was as though God had dropped me into a funnel and it was getting darker and darker. When I thought it couldn't get much darker, I hit the narrow part! Then, at the darkest hour, God dropped us out of the bottom of that funnel and everything became clear.

It was in the middle of a Thursday night when the dawn broke. Nothing changed circumstantially, but everything changed internally. I remember waking up with a sense of excitement and joy. Joanne awoke as well and wondered what was going on, but she too could sense something had taken place. There was a conscious awareness of God in a remarkable way. No audible voices or visions. God in His quiet and gentle way was renewing my mind. My thought process went something like this: *Neil, do you walk by faith or do you walk by sight? Are you walking by faith now? You believed Me last summer, do you believe Me now? Neil, do you love Me, or do you love My blessings? Do you worship Me for who I am, or do you worship Me for the blessings I bring? What if I suspended my conscious blessings in your life? Would you still believe in Me?*

I learned something that evening in a way I had never experienced before. In my spirit I responded, Lord, you know I love You, and I choose to walk by faith and not by sight. Lord, I worship You because of who You are regardless of the circumstances. I know that You will never leave me nor forsake me. Lord, I confess that I doubted your place in my life or questioned your ability to provide for all our needs.

Those precious moments can't be planned or predicted. They're not transferable. What we have previously learned from the Bible becomes incarnate during such times. Our worship is purified, and our love clarified. Faith moves from a textbook definition to a living reality. Trust is deepened when God puts us in a position where we have no other choice but to trust Him. We either learn to trust Him during those times or we end up compromising our faith. The Bible teaches us the rules of faith and knowledge of the object of our faith, but we learn to live by faith as we work out our salvation in fear and trembling. This is especially true when circumstances are not working favorably for us. The Lord has a way of stretching us through a knothole, and just before we are about to break in half, suddenly we slip through to the other side. But we will never go back to the same shape we were in before.

The next day everything changed. The Dean at Talbot School of Theology called to ask if I had taken any position yet. He asked me not to accept anything until we'd had the opportunity to talk. That Friday afternoon he offered me a faculty position, which I held for the next ten years. That same Friday evening a young man from the church I'd just left stopped by our home to see us at 10 p.m. When I asked him what he was doing here at that hour of the night, he said he wasn't sure. I invited him in and assured him that we would figure out something. I half jokingly asked him if he'd like to buy my house and he responded, "Maybe I would." The next Tuesday he came to our home with his parents and made an offer on our house that we accepted. Now we could sell our house *and* we knew the destination of our next move.

Nothing had changed externally before that morning, but everything changed internally. God can change in a moment what we can't change in a lifetime. Joanne and I had previously made a commitment not to make a major decision if we were emotionally and spiritually down. That alone has kept me from resigning after difficult board meetings or messages that bombed. The point is, never doubt in the darkness what God has clearly shown you in the light. We must keep on walking in the light of previous revelation. If it was true six months ago, it's still true. If we're serious about our walk with God, He will test us to determine if we love Him or His blessings. However, He may cloud the future so we learn to walk by faith and not by sight or feelings.

Understand that God has not left us, He has only suspended His "conscious" presence so that our faith will never rest on our feelings, or be established by unique experiences, or fostered by temporal blessings. If our physical parents found themselves in difficult circumstances and couldn't afford any Christmas presents when we were young, would we stop loving them? Would we stop looking to them for direction and support? If God's ministry of darkness should envelope you, keep on walking in the light of previous revelation.

Fortunately, I'd had some biblical preparation for this time of testing. What would you do if you were faithfully walking in the light and suddenly you found yourself engulfed in darkness? Job was enjoying the benefits of living righteously when, unexpectedly, it was all taken away. Health, wealth, and family were all gone! If we found ourselves in Job's shoes, our minds would likely spin with many questions:

"What did I do to deserve this?"

"Did I miss a turn in the road?"

"Is this what I get for living a righteous life?"

"Where is God?"

"God, why are You doing this to me?"

Like Job, we may even feel like cursing the day we were born. There were days I wasn't sure if we were going to make it. If it weren't for the message given in Isaiah 50:10–11 (NASB), I'm not sure we would have passed this test:

> *Who is among you that fears the Lord, that obeys the voice of His servant, that walks in darkness and has no light? Let him trust in the name of the Lord and rely on his God. Behold, all you who kindle a fire, who encircle yourselves with firebrands, walk in the light of your fire and among the brands you have set ablaze. This you will have from My hand: You will lie down in torment.*

Isaiah is talking about a believer, somebody who obeys God, and yet walks in darkness. Isaiah is not talking about the darkness of sin, nor even the darkness of this world (that is, the kingdom of darkness). He's talking about the darkness of uncertainty, a blanket of heaviness that hovers like a dark cloud over our very being. The assurances of yesterday have been replaced by the uncertainties of tomorrow. God has suspended His conscious blessings. Could this happen to a true believer? What is the purpose for such a dark time? What are followers of Christ to do when the path before them isn't certain?

In the light we can see the next step, the path ahead is clear. We know a friend from an enemy, and we can see where the obstacles are. The Word has been a lamp unto our feet. It directed our steps, but now we begin to wonder if it's true. Darkness has overcome us. We are embarrassed by how feeling-oriented we are. Every natural instinct says drop out, sit down, stop! But Isaiah encourages us to keep on living by faith according to what we know to be true.

Don't light your own fire is another lesson we must learn from Isaiah. In other words, don't create your own light. The natural tendency when we don't see it God's way, is to do it our way. Notice the text again, "Behold all you who kindle a fire, who encircle yourselves with firebrands, walk in the light of your fire…" God is not talking about the fire of judgment, He's talking about fire that creates light. Notice what happens when people create their own light, "…And among the brands you have set ablaze. This you will have from my hand: You will lie down in torment." Essentially God is saying, "Go ahead, do it your way. I will allow it, but misery will follow."

Let me illustrate this principle from earlier in the Bible. God called Abraham out of Ur into the Promised Land. In Genesis 22, a covenant was made in which God promised Abraham that his descendants would be more numerous than the sand on the seashore or the stars in the sky. Abraham lived his life in the light of that promise; then God turned out the light. So many months and years passed that his wife Sarah could no longer bear a child by natural means. God's promise had been so clear before, but now it looked like Abraham would have to assist God in its fulfillment. Who could blame Abraham for creating his own light? Sarah supplied the match by offering her handmaiden to Abraham. Out of that union came another nation, which has created so much conflict that the whole world lies down in torment. Jews and Arabs have not been able to dwell together peacefully to this day.

God superintended the birth of Moses and provided for his preservation. Raised in the home of Pharaoh, he was given the second most prominent position in Egypt. Then God put into his heart a burden to set his people free. Impulsively Moses pulled out his sword, attempting to help God, and God turned out the lights. Abandoned to the desert, Moses spent forty years tending his father-in-law's sheep. Then one day, Moses turned aside to see a burning bush that wasn't consumed. God turned the light back on.

I'm not suggesting that we may have to wait forty years for the cloud to lift. In our life span that would be more time than an average person's faith could endure. But the darkness may last for weeks, months, and possibly, in some exceptional cases, even years. God is in charge and He knows exactly how small a knothole He can pull us through. Isaiah wrote, "The One forming light and creating darkness, causing well-being and creating calamity; I am the Lord who does all these," (Isaiah 45:7 NASB). God does this for our good.

I almost created my own light during those two testing weeks. I looked into two ministry positions. One was with the research division of World Vision. It was a good position and I could have had it, but it required a lot of international travel and I couldn't do that to my family. The other was with Dr. Clyde Narramore and the Narramore Graduate School of Psychology. He had lost his faithful administrator of seventeen years, and I was interviewed to take his position. I could have had that position as well, but I knew I couldn't accept the offer. (The interview did pay dividends later.) Dr. Narramore had a syndicated radio ministry and he asked me to stand in for him when he traveled. The radio experience, however, was all honor and no honorarium.

The devil has a ministry of darkness that threatens to destroy us. God also has a ministry of darkness that purifies our faith. The devil tempts us with our destruction in mind. God tests us with our purification in mind. God was later to drop us into another funnel, but the second time would be much darker, and for a different purpose. The first led to my appointment at Talbot School of Theology. The second would be the birth of Freedom In Christ Ministries. In the meantime, off we went to seminary.

7

The Whole Gospel

I had just finished my doctorate in Institutional Management. Part of the curriculum taught me to plan, set goals, and make predictions for the future to ensure proper management. So how did such wisdom apply to me? I got up one morning dead broke, with no clue what my next step is, the phone rang and eight hours later I was a seminary professor! That gave new meaning to the Proverb, "The heart of man plans his way, but the Lord establishes his steps" (16:9 ESV). It wasn't my idea to be a seminary professor, so whose idea was it? Mind you, I wasn't disappointed. Actually I was excited, and grateful for the opportunity, but I was still dead broke.

I was driving another clunk of a car (a former Budget rental) that I bought from a Sears's parking lot. Sometime during that year of studies the reverse gear went out in the transmission. I had no money to fix it, so I had to park only where I could leave by driving forward. More than once I had to stick my foot out the door and push the car backwards. We had no insurance of any kind that year, which I don't advise, but there was no money except for bare necessities. We did a lot of praying.

When I left engineering to be a pastor, my salary dropped $10,000 a year. Becoming a seminary professor cost me another $10,000 a year in salary. Two more moves upward and I would have to pay someone in order to work! The young man who bought our house, couldn't come up with enough money for a down payment so I provided the second loan. There was equity in the house, but getting the cash would have to come later. Consequently, we had no choice but to rent a house.

I was still writing and defending my dissertation when the fall semester began. Pressure was on me to finish that degree since my appointment at the seminary was contingent upon it. My salary at the seminary was $18,000 a year, which we couldn't live on in Southern California, where the cost of living was far above the national average. I knew that was the case when I accepted the position, so I wasn't blaming anyone. I was counting on doing some pulpit supply work, or some other side ministry in order to support my family. So I was thankful that a request to speak at a church one Sunday morning came the first week that I was on campus. That Sunday I drove sixty miles to speak in a church, and they paid me $50. On the way home I was doing the math in my head. Fifty-two weeks times $50 equals? This was not going to work!

God doesn't only guide our steps, He meets all our needs. We started attending Granada Heights Friends Church, and they invited me to join their staff part time. I would preach Sunday evenings, and help with some counseling, which I did for the next four years. That provided enough income for us to survive. Sharing the pulpit with Verl Lindley, the founding pastor, was a privilege and learning experience. He was the best example of what a pastor should be that I have ever known. He would eventually retire after serving thirty-seven years in the church he started. He never suffered any church splits or scandals. He never wrote a book, and people didn't rush to get his sermon tapes. Nobody ever referred to the church as Verl Lindley's church. It was always Granada Heights Friends Church, built upon the character of the pastor, which should be the case for every church. Since I taught the core Pastoral Ministry class at Talbot, he was a great example for me to learn from.

What blessed me even more was the absence of any "prima donnas" in the church. There were no lay or staff people trying to exert their authority or influence. The church didn't attract such people. If social climbing, power-hungry people did attend the church, they probably realized by Verl's example that such practices would be frowned upon. They either left or learned to become servant leaders. The church and staff meetings were always peaceful. There was no need for *Robert's Rules of Order* to govern our behavior, since they didn't vote on anything. They practiced a process called "sensing." The moderator of the church would bring issues before the congregation and invite comments and questions to seek consensus. After a period of discussion the moderator would "sense" the direction God was leading, and make a decision reflecting that. If there was no consensus reached, the issue was tabled.

There was one issue, however, that couldn't be overlooked too much longer. The church was in organizational chaos, which I had no intention of interfering with. One Saturday morning I was attending a board meeting in which they were discussing the annual task of filling nearly 200 committee positions. They had twenty-seven committees, which is way too many for any church. Several leaders had been suggesting organizational changes that were sorely needed. The board had appointed a task force to look into the matter, but they had no power or authority to make any changes, and Verl wasn't even part of it. I never exerted myself in such meetings, but this time I felt led to say, "I only have fifteen hours a week to give you, and I don't think you are making best use of my time. Maybe you should let me help you with some master planning and organizational restructuring." The moderator thought that was an excellent suggestion, and asked all the staff to leave except Pastor Verl.

Two hours later the moderator called me and asked what I would recommend. I suggested that I meet with the pastoral staff first. We could have a two-day retreat and I would help them create a master plan for their own ministries. I knew I had to help Verl see the value of an organizational structure to accomplish our objectives or nothing would change. The church had just evolved over the years. It was a loving organism with no organization, which was quite the opposite from my first evangelical church experience. I also suggested that he dissolve the old task force and put together a new one composed of the most respected leaders of the church. Without the approval and participation of these leaders, nothing would change. Pastor Verl and I would also be on the task force.

I had learned a thing or two about change theory from my most recent experience. First, I couldn't throw caution to the wind, and second, I couldn't move any faster than I could educate. Six months later we had one board of elders overseeing seven committees. Each committee was responsible for their own area of ministry, which was clearly defined so there would be no turf wars. The committees could form sub-committees if that was necessary to fulfill their task. Every staff and committee member knew to whom they reported and what they were responsible for. During the process I repeatedly said that I had no interest in doing their planning for them, nor did I have any desire to run the church. My task was to show them how. It was a peaceful transition, with no opposition from the congregation. I looked carefully into a mirror, and to my delight I saw no bullet holes. Learning how to be a change agent, and understanding principles of leadership and management, were essential foundations for what lay ahead.

Meanwhile, at the seminary, I was appointed to oversee the chapel committee, which had no defined purpose. We would sing a song, give some announcements, and listen to a speaker, whom I had the privilege to select for the next eight years. Chapel met in the mornings, Tuesday through Thursday. Students had their own chapel on Friday, which was overseen by the student body president, who was on the chapel committee with me.

I had a lot of fun doing some creative events at chapel. Rather than seeing chapel as a mini church service, I saw it as an opportunity to expand the thinking of the student body and faculty. After chapel the teaching staff would informally meet for coffee in our lounge, and usually discuss the message they'd just heard. On Fridays they met for prayer while the students were having their chapel.

Several times I put together chapel series on controversial issues like women in ministry, Lordship salvation,[2] Christianity and politics, and so on. On the latter subject, I had a man give a message in the Thursday chapel entitled, "Why as a Christian I Am a Republican." For Wednesday chapel I asked an undergraduate professor who was a democrat, to give a "neutral" message on the biblical role that Christians should play politically. The following

2 "Lordship Salvation" implies that major changes should occur on conversion. The other extreme is "pure grace" where no evidence is necessary at the point of salvation.

Tuesday the chairman of the Political Science Department for Biola University, who was also the mayor of La Mirada, California, where the school was located, gave the message, "Why as a Christian I Am a Democrat." I invited all three to come to the student chapel for a panel discussion where the students could ask any questions they wanted. The faculty didn't want to miss this one since with one exception they were all right-wing Republicans. This was really fun!

In truth, I missed being a pastor the first couple of years that I taught at Talbot School of Theology. I was asked to candidate for a senior pastor position, but I had to say no for Joanne's sake. But that desire slowly changed, and I was content thinking that I had found my true calling. I was born to teach, but God had to deepen the life of the teacher in order to expand the message. The proper order in life should be character before career, maturity before ministry, and being before doing. Little did I know at the time that my most life-transforming events were yet to happen. How easy it would have been to rest on my laurels and coast through the rest of my life. God was not going to let that happen.

I came to Talbot with a burden. I believed in my heart that Jesus was the answer and that truth would set people free, but I hadn't observed that to the degree I thought was possible. I had seen many people come to Christ in my ministry, and there was a noticeable change after their conversion, but most continued to struggle with the same old issues. Where was the "new creation" in Christ? Where was the freedom that the gospel promised? And what about those spiritual conflicts that I encountered in ministry? These questions hounded me.

Burdened by the lack of substantive answers, I proposed a Master of Theology elective on Spiritual Warfare. Our seminary had never had such an elective, and there was some resistance to the idea. Dr. Clyde Narramore was the founder of Rosemead Graduate School of Psychology. He had given the psychology school to Biola University, and it was becoming a major graduate program at the university, along with Talbot School of Theology. Half the previous Rosemead faculty needed to be replaced, because they didn't fit the doctrinal profile the school required.

My first year at Talbot coincided with undergraduate missions professor Dr. Ed Murphy's last year of teaching at Biola University. He was a dear saint. In the previous year an undergraduate student had been experiencing some demonic manifestations. Ed was summoned to help her, which apparently fueled some opposition. Spearheaded by one of the professors at Rosemead, a policy was instituted that prohibited any exorcisms at Biola University. What kind of message did that send to the community? You can come to our school for your psychological needs, but not for your spiritual needs! Such a policy was possible under the previous President of Biola, but I don't think that would have happened under our new President, Dr. Clyde Cook. Before his appointment Dr. Cook had been chairman of the Undergraduate Missions Department and he had cross-cultural missionary experience.

Having a good relationship with Dr. Cook was an important asset in the years to come. There was a private country club in our vicinity that offered free golf privileges to 25 members of the clergy. Dr. Cook and I took advantage of this opportunity. We could only play when it wasn't busy and not on weekends. An undergraduate Bible professor named Nick Kurtanic also had this privilege and the three of us would enjoy each other's company when time allowed. My relationship with Nick, whose office was next to mine, would be invaluable during the darkest time of my life.

I knew I was breaking new ground with this elective, but I

was not going to rebel against the system. God has called all of us to be submissive to governing authorities, and I was not going to violate that clear instruction. There has never been a rebellious bone in my body. I knew that being submissive was necessary for our own spiritual protection. In addition, I didn't want to add to the confusion that often surrounds spiritual warfare ministries, or to be the cause for any disunity. I was blessed to have Dr. Robert Saucy as a friend. Dr. Saucy was the most respected man on campus, and the chairman of the Systematic Theology Department. As long as we were in agreement, nobody on campus would take much issue with me or with what I was doing. (Later he would serve on the board of Freedom In Christ Ministries for ten years. Years later we would write a book together on sanctification entitled *The Common Made Holy* (Harvest House, 1997), which I considered a real privilege.)

At the time there was not a lot of evangelical literature available on spiritual warfare. Some evangelicals saw the subject as a Pentecostal or charismatic issue and best suited for missions. I used Dr. Mark Bubeck's books, *The Adversary* and *Overcoming the Adversary* (Moody Press), for my initial texts. I came to know Mark as a friend later on. In those days there was only a handful of evangelical theologians speaking and writing on spiritual warfare, namely Dr. Fred Dickason, Dr. Victor Matthews, and Dr. Merrill Unger.

Eighteen students signed up the first time I taught the class, which is a very good number for a Master of Theology elective. It soon became the most popular elective at the seminary, with numbers nearly doubling every year. That first year I was very aware that what I *didn't* know was profound! I was just imparting information that I was reading from the Bible and other authors.

The Lord had to lead me through a number of paradigm shifts in order for my worldview to be anywhere near what the Bible was teaching.

Even to approach the subject of spiritual warfare I needed to understand the whole gospel, which I didn't fully comprehend at that time. I thoroughly studied the creation account and subsequent fall depicted in the first three chapters of Genesis. I needed to understand the nature of temptation and the role Satan played. The apostle John had written, "For all that is in the world, the lust of the flesh and the lust of the eyes and the boastful pride of life, is not from the Father, but is from the world" (1 John 2:16 NASB). Leaving out the context one could deduce from the passage that our battle was only against the world and the flesh.

Indeed the world and the flesh are formidable enemies, of which I was fully aware. Nobody had to convince me that I was living in a fallen world, and that I was still struggling with some old flesh patterns. My eyes were opened a little wider when I carefully looked at Genesis 3:6 (NSAB), "When the woman saw that the tree was good for food [lust of the flesh], and that it was a delight to the eyes [lust of the eyes], and that the tree was desirable to make one wise [boastful pride of life], she took from its fruit and ate; and she gave also to her husband with her, and he ate." The apostle John (see above) was describing three channels that Satan used to tempt Eve, which were exactly the same three channels that Satan used to tempt Jesus (see Matthew 4:1–10).

All I had seen were the channels that Satan used to tempt us, which would leave me battling myself, instead of the tempter. Satan's temptation of Eve questioned the will of God, the word of God, and the worship of God (Genesis 3:1–5).[3] I also came to

3 For a more detailed explanation of temptation read *The Bondage Breaker*, chapter seven (Anderson, Harvest House, second edition, 2000).

realize that all temptation is just an attempt to entice us to live our lives independently of God. Notice the temptation of Jesus in Matthew 4:1–4 (ESV):

> *Then Jesus was led up by the Spirit into the wilderness to be tempted by the devil. And after fasting forty days and forty nights, he was hungry. And the tempter came and said to Him, "If you are the Son of God, command these stones to become loaves of bread." But He answered, "It is written, 'Man shall not live by bread alone, but by every word that comes from the mouth of God.'"*

It was the Holy Spirit who led Jesus into the wilderness. It wasn't the devil. The devil probably wasn't looking forward to confronting Jesus. To make the odds a little more even, Jesus fasted forty days and nights and was hungry. When I fast for a day, I feel famished! This was a real temptation; Jesus was on the verge of starving to death. But what was the actual intent of Satan? He wanted Jesus to use His own divine attributes independently of the Father to save himself. He modeled a life that was totally dependent upon God the Father. Jesus came to give us an example to follow in His steps (1 Peter 2:21).

If that were all Jesus came to do, then he would be nothing more than a good moral example that we could imitate. The gospel is much more than that. "The Lord God formed the man of dust from the ground and breathed into his nostrils the breath of life, and the man became a living creature" (Genesis 2:7 ESV). He was physically alive, which meant that his soul was in union with his body. But Adam was also spiritually alive, which meant that his soul was in union with God. Consider Genesis 2:15–16 (ESV)

> *The Lord God took the man and put him in the garden of Eden to work it and keep it. And the Lord God commanded the man, saying, "You may surely eat of every tree of the garden, but of the tree of the knowledge of good and evil you shall not eat, for in the day that you eat of it you shall surely die."*

Eve was deceived, and Adam willfully chose to sin – and both died that very day. They didn't die physically; they died spiritually. Physical death would also be a consequence of sinning, but for Adam that wouldn't happen for another 900 plus years. What Adam and Eve lost in the fall was life. What Jesus came to give us was life. Such revelation opened up a new understanding of the gospel. Jesus said to Martha, "I am the resurrection and the life. Whoever believes in me, though he die, yet shall he live, and everyone who lives and believes in me shall never die. Do you believe this?" (John 11:25–26 ESV). In other words, if we die physically, we will continue to live spiritually.

This new insight changed my presentation of the gospel. Before I would say something like this, "Jesus is the Messiah who died for our sins. If we confess with our mouth that Jesus is Lord and believe in our heart that God raised Him from the dead, we will be saved. Then we will go to heaven when we die." That would give the impression that eternal life is something we get when we die, but that is not true. The apostle John wrote, "And this is the testimony, that God gave us eternal life, and this life is in His Son. Whoever has the Son has life; whoever does not have the Son of God does not have life" (1 John 5:11–12 ESV).

As a result of the fall, "you were dead in the trespasses and sins in which you once walked, following the course of this world, following the prince of the power of the air, the spirit that is now at work in the sons of disobedience" (Ephesians 2:1–2 ESV). We are all born into this world physically alive, but spiritually dead, that is, separated from God, because of sin. If you wanted to save a dead person and had the power to do it, what would you do? You would give life to that dead person. But if that was all you did, they would only die again.

To save a dead person, you have to perform two functions. First, you would have to cure the "disease" that caused them to die, and "…the wages of sin is death …" (Romans 6:23a). So Jesus went to the cross and died for our sins. Is that the whole gospel? No! Finish the verse, "…but the free gift of God is eternal life…" (Romans 6:23b ESV). I thank God for Good Friday, but what the Church celebrates every Easter is the new life we have in Christ because of His resurrection. Orthodox and Catholic Christians celebrate the resurrection every Sunday. Jesus is the bread of *life* (John 6:35). He is "the way, and the truth, and the *life*" (John 14:6). If you are a child of God, your name is written in the Lamb's book of *life* (Revelation 13:8).

I did some unofficial research and I discovered that most people attending evangelical churches did not know that. They knew John 10:10b (NKJV), "I have come that they may have life, and that they may have it more abundantly." But they believed the Lord was talking about their natural life and that Jesus came to make it better, which led some to embrace the prosperity gospel. That distortion of the gospel leads some to focus on physical healings and financial prosperity. When they are not physically healed and don't become wealthy they are disappointed in God, or beat themselves and others up for lack of faith.

The Church Fathers referred to salvation as union with God, which is what it is. In ancient Christian literature they never talked about being saved at some point of time in the past, as we commonly hear today. They understood that salvation for the believer began in their past when they were born-again, is presently being worked out, and will be completed in the future. In other words, we have been saved, we are being saved, and some day we shall be fully saved. All three verb tenses occur in the epistles and apply to believers. Nobody is completely saved until they are in a resurrected body and fully in the presence of Christ. I personally believe that born-again Christians should be assured of their salvation according to Ephesians 1:13–15 (ESV, emphasis added):

> *In Him you also, when you heard the word of truth, the gospel of your salvation, and believed in Him, were* sealed *with the promised Holy Spirit, who is the* guarantee *of our inheritance until we acquire possession of it, to the praise of His glory.*

The presence of the Holy Spirit in my life is my guarantee for the future, because I know He will never leave me or forsake me. What I had overlooked before were the often used prepositional phrases, "in Christ," or "in Him,' or "in the beloved," which all refer to the fact that believers are in union with God. Forty such phrases occur in the six chapters of Ephesians alone. Before Christ, I was "in Adam," or "in the flesh," but now I am alive "in Christ." The apostle Paul makes this clear in Romans 8:9 (ESV), "You, however, are not in the flesh but in the Spirit, if in fact the Spirit of God dwells in you. Anyone who does not have the Spirit of Christ does not belong to Him."

Even if you knew that the gospel included forgiveness and new life in Christ, you are still a third short of the whole gospel. Adam and Eve were created to rule over the birds of the sky, the beasts of the field, and the fish of the sea (Genesis 1:26). That dominion was for them and their descendants. They forfeited that when they sinned and Satan became the rebel holder of authority. Jesus referred to Satan as the ruler of this world (John 16:11), and said that the whole world lies in the power of the evil one (1 John 5:19). So what did Jesus come to do? "The reason the Son of God appeared was to destroy the works of the devil" (1 John 3:8 ESV).

The other third of the gospel is what most of the world is waiting to hear. Many western Christians are not aware that the dominant religion of the world is spiritism. When I travel to Third World countries the disarming of Satan is the "good news" that they are waiting to hear. Spiritists will prepare baskets of fruit or some other offering to appease the deities. They visit their shamans and quack doctors hoping to manipulate the spiritual world. New Age proponents do the same thing. We have the privilege to present a whole gospel that is summarized in Colossians 2:13–15 (ESV):

> *And you, who were dead in your trespasses and the uncircumcision of your flesh, God made alive together with him, having forgiven us all our trespasses, by canceling the record of debt that stood against us with its legal demands. This He set aside, nailing it to the cross. He disarmed the rulers and authorities and put them to open shame, by triumphing over them in Him.*

Understanding the whole gospel changed how I taught evangelism, how I did ministry, and most important it changed how I perceived myself and other believers. I was about to discover who I really am.

8

A New Identity

I had been a farm boy, a migrant farm worker, a sea and rescue swimmer, an electronics technician, a wrestling coach, an aerospace engineer, a campus pastor, a youth pastor, a college pastor, a minister of Christian Education, a senior pastor, and now I was a seminary professor. I was 42 years old and I still didn't fully know who I was. I had derived my identity from my natural heritage and work. Mentally I was slowly turning the corner to a greater understanding of who I was and how that affected the way I lived. I came to an interesting conclusion. It is not what we do that determines who we are. Who we are determines what we do. So who are we? How one answers that question reveals one's belief about the very essence of life.

If you think it is a superficial question, try asking others, "Who are you?" I did, and I got some very puzzled looks. Some would say their name. "Come on, you know me, I'm Bob Smith!" To which I would answer, "That is just your name. Who are you?" Some would share their journey. "I am just a traveler through time hoping to improve my life and others'." Many would share negative expressions of themselves. "I'm just a nobody," or "I'm a loser." In one seminary class I asked a related question. "Suppose I got to know you personally, would I like you?" One student said out loud, "You would feel sorry for me!" He probably said that in jest, but maybe not.

As a pastor who did a lot of counseling I had already discovered that most people don't inherently feel good about themselves. Becoming a Christian didn't necessarily change their self-perception. Realizing how widespread the problem was, I read some psychological articles and books about self-esteem. Psychology by definition means a study of the soul, which is part of any systematic theology. Secular psychology, however, only takes into account the natural person, and has no understanding of God, the spiritual realm, or the person God intended us to be. Lacking any spiritual dimension, the understanding and conclusions of secular psychology would be very different from those of biblical psychology or anthropology. Secularists can provide a psychological profile of your personality, but that is very different from the essence of who we are as human beings created in the image of God.

Self-help psychology may lead to some form of self-actualization, but it ends with humans trying to make a name for themselves. Stroking one another's egos and picking yourself up by your own bootstraps has no lasting effect on one's self-perception. M. Raymond wrote:

> *Specialists in the material sciences cannot help us. Psychologists who are not also real philosophers will be greater hindrances than helpers. And the psychologist-philosopher, if he is to be of any real assistance, will have to be something of a theologian; for this question about who you are as a human being cannot*

> *be answered without touching the Divine. Therefore, the only "ology" that can ever give proper reply to the question "Who are you?" is theology – a theology that teaches that each of us is a child of God who, under God's loving guidance and with God's generous help, is working out a God-given destiny.* [4]

Understanding the whole gospel provided the answer I was looking for. The eternal spiritual life we receive when we are born again is what determines who we are. "But to all who did receive Him, who believed in his name, he gave the right to become children of God" (John 1:12 ESV). Being a child of God is the basis for becoming the person He intended us to be as the apostle John explains in 1 John 3:1–3 (ESV):

> *See what kind of love the Father has given to us, that we should be called children of God; and so we are. The reason why the world does not know us is that it did not know Him. Beloved, we are God's children now, and what we will be has not yet appeared; but we know that when he appears we shall be like him, because we shall see Him as he is. And everyone who thus hopes in Him purifies himself as He is pure.*

I had some basic knowledge of these passages, but the truth had not fully entered into my heart. Then one incredible day it did. I don't even remember what brought about the change. All I can say is, "Where once I was blind, now I see." I may have known what the Bible said about our identity in Christ, but why hadn't

4 *Spiritual Secrets of a Trappist Monk*, by M. Raymond, Father, OCSO, Sophia Institute Press, 2000, page 9. Joanne gave me this book for Christmas in 2010. It was like I was reading my own message, but from a Catholic perspective. I was thrilled that Catholics could receive the same understanding of who we are in Christ. I only hope that many read it.

I fully appropriated that reality before? Having an intellectual knowledge of something doesn't always translate into an inner reality. Somehow the truth has to be incarnated. Other key figures in church history had the same experience. The following is a testimony by Watchman Nee:[5]

> *For years after my conversion I had been taught to reckon [consider oneself to be dead to sin and alive in Christ]. I reckoned from 1920 to 1927. The more I reckoned that I was dead to sin, the more alive I clearly was. I simply could not believe myself dead, and I could not produce the death. Whenever I sought help from others I was told to read Romans 6:11, and the more I read Romans 6:11 and tried to reckon, the further away death was; I could not get it. I fully appreciated the teaching that I must reckon, but I could not make out why nothing resulted from it. I have to confess that for months I was troubled. I said to the Lord, "If this is not clear, if I cannot be brought to see this which is so very fundamental, I will cease to do anything. I will not preach any more; I will not serve Thee any more; I want first of all to get thoroughly clear here." For months I was seeking and at times I fasted, but nothing came through.*
>
> *I remember one morning – that morning was a real morning and one, I can never forget – I was upstairs sitting at my desk reading the Word and praying, and I said, "Lord, open my eyes!" And then in a flash I saw it. I saw my oneness with Christ. I saw that I was in Him, and that when He died I died. I saw that the question of my death was a matter of the past, and not of the future, and that I was just as truly dead as He was because I was in Him when He died.*

5 Watchman Nee, *The Normal Christian Life* (Wheaton, Ill: Tyndale House Publishers, 1977), pp. 64–65.

Watchman Nee was referring to Romans 6:11, "So you must consider [reckon] yourselves dead to sin and alive to God in Christ Jesus." Considering it so, doesn't make it so. You consider it so, because it is so. If you think reckoning makes you dead to sin, you will reckon yourself into a wreck. Death is the ending of a relationship, but not an existence. Sin is still present, and physical death is still imminent, but our relationship with both has changed forever, because we are alive "in Christ."

A pastor paid me a visit and said, "I have been in the ministry for twenty-three years and it has been a continuous personal struggle. I listened to one of your messages and I think I finally understand. Then I read Colossians 3:3, 'For you have died, and your life is hidden with Christ in God.' That's it, isn't?" I assured him that it was and then he asked, "How do I do that?" I asked him to read the passage again a little more slowly. "For you *have* died…" For twenty-three years this precious man had been trying to become somebody he already was. The same happened to Hudson Taylor:[6]

> *I felt the ingratitude, the danger, the sin of not living nearer to God. I prayed, agonized, strove, and made resolutions, read the Word more diligently, sought more time for meditation – but all without avail. Every day, almost every hour, the consciousness of sin oppressed me.*
>
> *I knew that if I could abide in Christ all would be well, but I could not… Each day brought its register of sin and failure, of lack of power. To will was indeed present within me, but how to perform I found not… I hated myself, my sin, yet gained no strength against it… I felt I was a child of God…*

6 Dr. and Mrs. Howard Taylor, *Hudson Taylor's Spiritual Secret* (Chicago: Moody Press, 1990), pp. 158–64.

But to rise to my privileges as a child, I was utterly powerless.

When my agony of soul was at its height, a sentence in a letter from dear McCarthy was used to remove the scales from my eyes, and the Spirit of God revealed to me the truth of our oneness with Jesus as I had never known it before. (I quote from memory): "But how to get faith strengthened? Not by striving after faith, but by resting on the Faithful One."

As I read, I saw it all! "If we believe not, He abideth faithful." I looked to Jesus and saw (and when I saw, oh, how the joy flowed!) that He had said, "I will never leave thee." I thought, I have striven in vain to rest in Him. I'll strive no more...

I am no better than before. In a sense I do not wish to be. But I am dead, buried with Christ – aye, and risen to! And now Christ lives in me and "the life that I now live in the flesh, I live by the faith of the Son of God, who loved me and gave Himself for me.

Such was my experience. In the paragraph cited above Hudson Taylor was referring to Galatians 2:20 (ESV), "I have been crucified with Christ. It is no longer I who live, but Christ who lives in me. And the life I now live in the flesh I live by faith in the Son of God, who loved me and gave himself for me." I wanted to share that verse with everyone, but the response was often, "Ya, I know!" But I could tell by their demeanor that they didn't know in a liberating way. They knew the verse, but not the truth. I didn't question their salvation, because I had become a Christian and served God for years before my eyes were fully opened to the truth of who I am in Christ. Without this revelation I could never write the books I have written, nor have the ministry I now have.

Christ promised to meet all our needs, and the most critical needs are the "being" needs such as forgiveness and eternal life, as well as our acceptance, security, and significance. I tried to show how He does that in my book, *Who I Am In Christ*.[7] The chapter titles are as follows:

The Believer's Identity in Christ

I am accepted:

John 1:12	I am God's child
John 15:15	I am Jesus' chosen friend
Romans 5:1	I have been made holy and accepted by God (justified)
1 Corinthians 6:17	I am united with the Lord and one with Him in spirit
1 Corinthians 6:20	I have been bought with a price –I belong to God
1 Corinthians 12:27	I am a member of Christ's body, part of His family
Ephesians 1:1	I am a saint, a holy one
Ephesians 1:5	I have been adopted as God's child
Ephesians 2:18	I have direct access to God through the Holy Spirit
Colossians 1:14	I have been bought back (redeemed) and forgiven of all my sins
Colossians 2:10	I am complete in Christ

7 Anderson, Neil, *Who I Am In Christ*, (Ventura, CA, Regal Books, 2001).

I am secure:

Romans 8:1–2	I am free from condemnation
Romans 8:28	I am assured that all things work together for good
Romans 8:31f	I am free from any condemning charges against me
Romans 8:35f	I cannot be separated from the love of God
2 Corinthians 1:21–22	I have been established, anointed, and sealed by God
Colossians 3:3	I am hidden with Christ in God
Philippians 1:6	I am sure that the good work that God has started in me will be finished
Philippians 3:20	I am a citizen of heaven
2 Timothy 1:7	I have not been given a spirit of fear, but of power, love, and a sound mind
Hebrews 4:16	I can find grace and mercy in time of need
1 John 5:18	I am born of God and the evil one cannot touch me

I am significant:

Matthew 5:13–16	I am the salt and light for everyone around me
John 15:1, 5	I am a part of the true vine, joined to Christ and able to produce much fruit
John 15:16	I have been handpicked by Jesus to bear fruit
Acts 1:8	I am a personal witness of Christ's
1 Corinthians 3:16	I am God's temple where the Holy Spirit lives

2 Corinthians 5:17f	I am at peace with God and he has given me the work of making peace between himself and other people. I am a minister of reconciliation
2 Corinthians 6:1	I am God's co-worker
Ephesians 2:6	I am seated with Christ in the heavenly realm
Ephesians 2:10	I am God's workmanship
Ephesians 3:12	I may approach God with freedom and confidence
Philippians 4:13	I can do all things through Christ who strengthens me

I handed out that outline to students, friends, and people God was sending my way for counseling. The responses were all over the map. Some said they didn't think that list described them. Others asked, "Is this really true?" Some cried. One lady who was under heavy demonic oppression threw the paper down, and wanted to leave the room. The last thing the devil wants you to know is who you are in Christ. One of my students who had a college ministry said, "I don't think my college students will be interested in this, and, frankly, I can't see the relevance!" He was not known for his humility. The proud want to make a name for themselves. For the last several years Freedom In Christ Ministries has made the list available as a bookmark. Millions have been sold. They are taped to refrigerators all over the country, and the interest hasn't waned.

I offered a Saturday seminar on Spiritual Identity at Granada Heights Friends Church. I really didn't care how many came. I offered it more for my own understanding. I wanted to see what the public reaction would be to this seminal truth. Most were blown away, and wondered why they had never heard this before. Twenty-five years later we still get that question.

The above list made its way to a local pastor whose theological education was similar to mine. I suspect that someone in his church showed him the list. He proceeded to write a very condemning article about me that has made the rounds ever since. Someone from the church was deeply bothered by his pastor's actions, and asked me to call him, which I did. I asked him what his primary concern was. The primary objection was to my belief that Christians are identified as saints, or righteous ones, or holy ones. He said, "If I told my congregation who they are in Christ, that would take away their motivation to stop sinning." In my ministry I have experienced just the opposite.

This man was supposed to be a good Bible teacher. I said, "So it's your choice to not tell them who they really are in Christ, and to motivate them out of guilt and shame?" The concerned parishioner told me later that the church board went over the pastor's head and hired a pastoral counselor, since nobody would go to see this "Bible teacher." How would you like to have this man as your pastor? He later fired the staff person they hired to do pastoral care. How could you be a good Bible teacher and tell them not to believe what Scripture says about them? How can a godly pastor motivate people with fear and condemnation, when there is "no condemnation for those who are in Christ Jesus" (Romans 8:1) and "no fear in love, but perfect love casts out fear. For fear has to do with punishment, and whoever fears has not been perfected in love" (1 John 4:18 ESV)?

Knowing who we are in Christ is personally liberating, and it greatly influences how we do ministry. Mike Quarles, the number one stockbroker in Birmingham, Alabama, was going through this inner transformation at the same time I was. He would later join our ministry. He had cocktail parties in his 4,000-square-foot home overlooking the city. The partying and drinking caught up with him, however, and he suffered a breakdown. During treatment someone shared Christ with him and he was born again. He was zealous about his new-found faith, and wanted to tell everyone about it. He told me once, "If you tied an average Baptist to my leg I would have dragged him to death!" He sensed a call to go into ministry, but as soon as he was accepted at a seminary, his wife left him. A year later he met Julia, who had suffered the loss of her first husband to an untimely death. They got married and off they went to seminary. After graduation, he accepted a call to be a Presbyterian pastor. He continued with the same zeal, and burned out. He realized that what he was teaching wasn't working for him. So he resigned his pastorate and went back to his old trade of selling stocks.

Mike became a hopeless alcoholic. Later we would write a book together entitled, *Freedom From Addiction* (Regal Books, 1996). In the book he lists twenty-five things he tried that didn't work. He would sit in those recovery circles and say, "Hi, I'm Mike. I'm an alcoholic." He almost choked the first time he said that, but he had to say it if he wanted to stay in treatment. Then one day his eyes were opened to who he is in Christ and he never drank again. He wasn't an alcoholic, he was a child of God. He was alive in Christ and dead to sin.

Meanwhile, I was providing free counseling at Granada Heights Friends Church as well as at the seminary. I began to notice that every inquirer who came to see me had one thing in common. None of them knew who they were in Christ, nor did they understand what it meant to be a child of God. If the Holy

Spirit is bearing witness with our spirit that we are children of God (Romans 8:16), why weren't they sensing that? That is still true for everyone I meet with around the world.

Why don't we know who we are? That question dogged me for years. Is this a conscious realization that we grow into, and therefore part of the growth process? That seemed to fit my experience. Or did God intend this truth to be the foundation from which we grow. If you search Scripture, which I did, you have to come to the conclusion that our identity and position in Christ is foundational. The apostle Paul taught that we need to be firmly rooted in Christ in order to grow in Christ, and see to it that we are not carried away by human traditions and elementary principles of the world (Colossians 2:6–10).

I concluded that there were two primary reasons why every Christian isn't fully aware of their identity in Christ. First, the truth can't set you free if you don't know it. Pastors like the one I mentioned earlier in this chapter are contributing to the blinding. If you have been told all your life that you are just a no-good sinner saved by grace, you will probably believe it, and your behavior will reinforce the belief. If you sin, you must be a sinner. That would be true if what you do determines who you are. Then every time you sneeze, you must be a sneezer, and those who burp must be burpers. The infinite wisdom of God foresaw such faulty conclusions and inspired the apostle Paul to write in Ephesians 1:16–18 (ESV):

> *I do not cease to give thanks for you, remembering you in my prayers, that the God of our Lord Jesus Christ, the Father of glory, may give you a spirit of wisdom and of revelation in the knowledge of Him, having the eyes of your hearts enlightened,*

> *that you may know what is the hope to which He has called you, what are the riches of His glorious inheritance in the saints.*

The second reason is the lack of repentance. The prayer above asks that we may have a true knowledge of God, having the eyes of our hearts enlightened to know who we are, that is, our identity in Christ. I would later learn that a true knowledge of God and true knowledge of who we are in Christ is the real basis for mental health. Let me illustrate how the lack of repentance can distort our knowledge of God. About the time that I discovered who I was, a pastor's wife was referred to me. She was suffering emotionally and mentally. She was plagued by bizarre thoughts that made false associations: she couldn't wear a red dress, because that was the color of Jesus' blood, or she couldn't buy some object at a grocery store, because that would cause a curse to fall upon her four-year-old son. I listened for half an hour and said, "You really love Jesus, don't you?" "Oh, yes," she said. "He is my savior." Then I asked, "You really love the Holy Spirit, don't you?" "Oh, He is my comforter," she answered. I continued, "But you don't love God the Father, do you?" She didn't answer directly, but her tears said it all.

She grew up with a verbally abusive mother, but that wasn't her primary struggle. She was more upset with her father. He never did anything for or against her. He just sat and watched his wife abuse their daughter and didn't do anything to protect her. She believed that God the Father was like that. Jesus did something. He marched to the cross and died for our sins, and was resurrected so that we could have new life. The Holy Spirit comforts her, or so she thought. Actually she was under demonic oppression, which is where the bizarre thoughts were coming from. God the Father just sits on his throne like a lump and doesn't do anything, or so she thought. Realizing that she had a distorted image of God, I gave her a set of recordings by A.W. Tozer on the attributes of God. I asked her to listen to them, and she did; three times.

The impact was zero, which really raised some questions for me. I was chairman of the Practical Theology Department and I deeply believed in the teaching and preaching of God's Word. I gave this lady some of the best teaching available that should have impacted her, but it produced no results at all. My commitment to teach and preach never wavered, but I knew something more than the verbal communication of God's Word had to happen if God's children were going to be free of their past and become the persons God intended them to be.

Most of her bizarre thoughts were centered around her four-year-old child. I believe the Lord led me to ask her, "Is your husband the biological father of that child?" He wasn't! Now that we knew the root of the problem, we were able to work toward proper resolution.

I would spend the rest of my days at Talbot learning how God's children could be established alive and free in Christ.

Every born-again believer is a child of God and free in Christ, but how many are living that way? Jesus said we need to "repent and believe the gospel" (Mark 1:15). How to help someone genuinely repent in a liberating way was still part of my learning process. To help the belief process I wrote the following analogy:

Slavery in the United States was abolished by the Thirteenth Amendment on December 18, 1865. How many slaves were there on December 19? In reality, none, but many still lived like slaves, because they never learned the truth. Others heard the good news, but continued living as they had always been taught and thus maintained their negative self-image.

The plantation owners were devastated by this proclamation of emancipation. *We're ruined! Slavery has been abolished. We've lost the battle to keep our slaves.* But their chief spokesman slyly responded, *Not necessarily. As long as these people think they're still slaves, the proclamation of emancipation will have no practical effect. We don't have any legal right over them anymore, but many don't know it. Keep your slaves from learning the truth, and your control over them will not even be challenged.*

But what if the news spreads?

Don't panic. We have another barrel on our gun. We may not be able to keep them from hearing the news, we still have the potential to deceive the whole world. They don't call me the father of lies for nothing. Just tell them that they misunderstood the Thirteenth Amendment. Tell them that they are going to be free, not that they are free already. The truth they heard is just positional truth, not actual truth. Someday they may receive the benefits, but not now.

But they'll expect us to say that. They won't believe us.

Then pick out a few persuasive ones of their own who are convinced that they're still slaves and let them do the talking for you. Remember, most of these newly freed people were born slaves and have lived like slaves all their lives. All we have to do is to deceive them so that they still think like slaves. As long as they continue doing what slaves do, it will not be hard to convince them that they must still be slaves. They will maintain their slave identity because of the things they do. The moment they try to confess that they are no longer slaves, just whisper in their ears, "How can you even think you are no longer a slave when you are doing things that slaves do?" After all, we also have the capacity to accuse the brethren day and night.

Years later, many slaves have still not heard the wonderful news that they have been freed, so naturally they continue to live the way they have always lived. Some slaves have heard the good news, but they evaluate it by what they are presently doing and feeling. They reason, *I'm still living in bondage, doing the same things I have always done. My experience tells me that I must not be free. I'm feeling the same way I was before the proclamation, so it must not be true. After all, your feelings always tell the truth.* So they continue to live according to how they feel, not wanting to be hypocrites.

One former slave hears the good news, and receives it with great joy. He checks out the validity of the proclamation, and finds out that the highest of all authorities originated the decree. Not only that, but it personally cost that authority a tremendous price, which he willingly paid so that the slaves could be free. As a result, the slave's life is transformed. He correctly reasons that it would be hypocritical to believe his feelings and not the truth. Determined to live by what he knows to be true, his experience begins to change rather dramatically. He realizes that his old master has no authority over him and does not need to be obeyed. He gladly serves the one who set him free.

9

The Truth Encounter

During my second year teaching at the seminary, I had a pivotal counseling session with an undergraduate coed student. She was a victim of child abuse, and seven years of counseling hadn't resolved anything. She had a surreal ability to point out sins in others. As far as I could tell, she was right. Was this a gift from God? I suspected not, so I approached the problem from a spiritual counterfeit perspective. Suddenly she sprang out of her chair, reached across my desk to grab a pencil, and raked it across her wrists. It did break the skin, but no blood vessels. I managed to get the pencil away from her, and calm her down. Later I prayed, "Dear God, there must be a better way than this to help such people!"

The next time we met, I asked my secretary to sit in on the session. The inquirer[8] started telling me everything her counselor at Rosemead was going to say and do that afternoon when she met with him for counseling. She was telling me this with a smile on her face. I said, "You like that don't you? You like having that

8 In our ministry we refer to ourselves as encouragers and the ones seeking help as inquirers.

kind of power over others, don't you?" As soon as I said that, an evil spirit manifested and challenged me. I told it to leave in the name of Jesus and the spirit said, "Where will I go?" My frightened secretary said out loud, "Not here!"

The school had a policy that prohibited me from helping her, and I was not going to be out from under God's protection by rebelling against established authority. So I immediately called the school President. I said, "Dr. Cook, I have an undergraduate student in my office who has a demonic problem. The school has a policy prohibiting me from helping her, what would you like me to do?" He said, "Stay on the line, the Dean of Students is in my office, and I want you to talk to him." I explained the situation, and he said, "You help her, and we'll pray." The next day they tore up the policy.

Given that it was a controversial issue on campus, I advised the coed inquirer to defer all questions to me should someone ask what happened to her. Questions would be inevitable since she had been set free from the oppression, and she looked like a totally different person. I was able to ascertain that the source of her problem was unforgiveness. When we helped her forgive her parents, submit to God, and resist the devil she walked out free. For the first time in her life she had mental peace. She told me that the quietness in her mind bothered her at first. Those "voices" in her head were the only companions she had. They were also the source for her ability to know the sins in others. She could no longer do that after her new-found freedom. What she'd thought was a gift from God, was just an evil spirit. It is interesting to note that when Jesus pointed out the evil intentions of the Pharisees, they accused Him of having a demon (John 7:20; 48–49). They assumed such esoteric knowledge had to come from a supernatural source. They didn't know they were talking to the Son of God who knew the thoughts and intentions of their hearts.

The coed had a part-time job working as a secretary in the undergraduate missions department. Her boss was the Dean of the department. He noticed the change immediately and asked what had happened. He called me the next day and said, "My secretary said I am supposed to talk to you." The three of us had lunch together, and he, being a cultural anthropologist, proceeded to offer a cultural explanation for her change. The coed looked quizzically at me, and I was able to silently advise her to say nothing. The Dean never once asked what I had done to help her.

We all see life from our own perspective. The medical doctors had seen her problem as a chemical imbalance and had given her a prescription. The psychologist was using Cognitive Behavior Therapy (CBT) to treat her psychological disorder. The pastors saw only the flesh patterns she exhibited. Their perspectives weren't wrong, just incomplete. Wisdom is seeing life from God's perspective, and that was what I was searching for. Such revelation, however, was slow in coming.

Ironically the Rosemead professor who'd pushed through the policy came to my office two years later in a frenzy, and said, "It happened, right in my office!" I asked, "What happened?" He had witnessed some kind of demonic manifestation in one of his clients, and it had freaked him out. I encouraged him to calm down. We talked over the case and I made some suggestions. He went from being an unbeliever to being a believer in the spiritual world, and then left his faculty position. I'm not sure why, but I suspect he didn't want to be part of any controversy.

How does one resolve spiritual conflicts? All I knew at that time was the classic power encounter. The pastor or missionary calls up the demon. Some will try to get the demon's name and spiritual rank, and try to cast it out. I tried that a few times, and there was an ugly confrontation that left one wondering who was more powerful. Even worse, it didn't last.

One Sunday afternoon a pastoral friend called and said, "We are in a spiritual battle over here, please pray for us." I could hear the naming and claiming going on and the demonic screams in the background. I did pray for them, and two hours later I received another call. "She's free, praise God and hallelujah." When I hung up I said to Joanne, "I'll get another call within a couple of days." Sure enough, the phone rang the next day and the pastor said, "Please pray, we are at it again!"

At the time I knew there was something wrong with this scenario, but what? The devil is supposed to be disarmed. The battle has already been won. Why are we trying to accomplish what God has already done? I started to see a pattern of faulty thinking that was plaguing the Church. We try to put the old self to death, when he is already dead (Romans 6:6). We seek more power, when we already have all we need (Ephesians 1:18–19). We try to defeat the devil, when Jesus has already disarmed him (Colossians 2:15). We try to do for ourselves and others what God has already done for us. Such thinking is similar to the Galatian heresy (Galatians 3:1–3 ESV):

> *O foolish Galatians! Who has bewitched you? It was before your eyes that Jesus Christ was publicly portrayed as crucified. Let me ask you only this: Did you receive the Spirit by the works of the law or by hearing with faith? Are you so foolish? Having begun by the Spirit, are you now being perfected by the flesh?*

We are saved by faith, we live by faith, and we are sanctified by faith. So the real issue is not how to behave, but what to believe. So what do we believe about the spiritual world and how do we engage it?

That boring Bible study I did on Wednesday evenings on the kingdom of God years earlier started bearing fruit. It helped me move away from western rationalism and naturalism to a more biblical worldview. When you realize there are two kingdoms, one of darkness and one of light it changes how you read the Bible. These two kingdoms are in conflict. It is a battle between good and evil, between true prophets and false prophets, between the Spirit of truth, and the father of lies, between Christ and the anti-Christ, and we are part of this conflict whether we like it or not. It started in the Garden of Eden and continues through the end times depicted in the Book of Revelation. Every movement of God to free His people is challenged from the birth of the first deliverer, Moses, to the birth of *the* deliverer, Jesus. Herod ordered all male children under two years of age to be killed in order to prevent the birth of Christ. Satan filled the heart of Judas to betray Christ, which backfired, because it played right into the hand of God.

When Adam sinned, Satan became the god of this world. Two sovereigns cannot rule in the same sphere at the same time, especially when they are diametrically opposed to each other. To resolve this issue Jesus selected the twelve disciples who followed Him around for at least a year to observe His example. Then "He called the twelve together and gave them power and authority over all demons and to cure diseases, and He sent them out to proclaim the kingdom of God and to heal" (Luke 9:1–2 ESV). Then He chose 72 others to do the same thing. "The seventy-two returned with joy, saying, 'Lord, even the demons are subject to us in your name'" (Luke 10:17 ESV). Jesus cautioned them not to rejoice in that, but to rejoice that their names are written in heaven. I received that as a caution for myself, and continued focusing on the answer (Jesus) and not the problem.

I noticed that the first thing Jesus did was to give them power and authority over demons and that is what caused them to be joyful. Whoever has the authority has the right to rule, whereas power is the ability to rule. Such teaching had been absent in my earlier seminary education. I was taught the great commission in Matthew 28:19–20 (ESV), "Go therefore and make disciples of all nations, baptizing them in the name of the Father and of the Son and of the Holy Spirit, teaching them to observe all that I have commanded you. And behold, I am with you always, to the end of the age." Every missionary knows that verse, but not everyone knows the verse before it and why it is so significant. Jesus said: "All authority in heaven and on earth has been given to Me. Go therefore …" (28:18b ESV)

Satan has no authority on earth. I wondered how many Christians knew that? Jesus has the authority, because He is God, but what about His children? If you are just a sinner saved by grace you will likely see yourself as a powerless victim caught between two opposing powers, and will likely fear Satan more than God. But that isn't who you are. Satan is disarmed; God is all powerful, and you are a child of God, a joint heir with Jesus, and seated with Christ in heavenly places (Ephesians 2:6 ESV). Jesus is seated at the right hand of God, which is the source of all authority, and that is the spiritual position of every believer. You cannot delegate responsibility without authority, and this power *and* authority has been conveyed upon us to continue the work of Christ. We have the authority to do God's will, and we have the power as long as we live by the Spirit, which is the apostle Paul's point in Ephesians 6:10 (ESV): "Finally, be strong in the Lord and in the strength of His might." We have no spiritual authority to do our own will, and we have no power if we live by the flesh. It all depends on our identity and position in Christ. Under the New Covenant we live by faith according to what God says is true in the power of the Holy Spirit and then we won't carry out the desires of the flesh (Galatians 5:16).

A local professional counselor called me at the seminary and said, "I have never given any place for the demonic, but I have a client who may have such a problem. Could you meet with us to provide some assessment?" Four years of counseling and a battery of tests had resulted in nothing. She was covered with self-inflicted wounds. It took me less than a minute to discern her problem, and I said to her, "There is a spiritual battle going on for your mind." She said, "Praise God, someone finally understands."

The next week she came to see me. She was a large lady who always wore sweatshirts to cover her scars. Ten minutes into our conversation she got out of her chair and started walking toward me with a menacing look. What would you do? I could tell by her eyes that another spirit had taken over. I calmly said to the evil spirit, "I'm a child of God, you cannot touch me," which is a paraphrase of 1 John 5:18. I said, "Sit down," and she did.

The authority we have in Christ does not increase with the volume of our voice. We don't shout out the devil. In that sense it is no different than parental authority. If we scream and yell at our children trying to maintain some control we are not exercising our God-given authority as parents. We are actually undermining it. We are responding in the flesh instead of calmly taking our place in Christ. It may bring about some temporal results, but not anything of lasting value, and we lose some respect in the process.

Knowing that believers had such power and authority over the kingdom of darkness changed the nature of the conflict, but I still didn't know how to set them free. The classic model of deliverance was confrontational, yet dialoguing with demons had detrimental effects, the first being deception. Demons all speak from their own nature and they are all liars. If you believe what they say, you will likely be deceived. Second, the inquirer is totally being bypassed. They will have no recall of anything that took place during the session. Therefore nothing has really changed in the life of the believer. Third, all the work is being done by the "exorcist." Fourth, demons are manifested instead of God. God isn't being glorified, Satan is. The glory of God is a manifestation of His presence – and He does everything decently and in order. We glorify God by bearing much fruit, and maintaining self-control, which is a fruit of the Spirit.

The power-encounter method was derived from the gospels, with little attention given to the epistles. Before the cross, Satan was not disarmed. It would take some specially endowed authority agent to confront the demons, which was Christ. He conferred that authority upon the twelve and then upon the seventy-two. After the cross and resurrection, Satan is disarmed. Since Pentecost every believer has the power and authority to do God's will, because every child of God has the same position in Christ, and is possessed by the same Holy Spirit. It is no longer the outside agent's responsibility. Every child of God has to submit to God and resist the devil themselves (James 4:7), which is why there are no instructions in the epistles to cast a demon out of anyone. Christians must know their identity and position in Christ, and know that they have the authority and power to stand firm, resist the devil, and do God's will. Pastors have the responsibility to teach that to their congregations, but it is the congregation's responsibility to live accordingly.

People's lives are like a house where the garbage hasn't been taken out in months. It is going to attract a lot of flies. Initially I was trying to get rid of the flies instead of getting rid of the garbage. One could study the flight patterns of the flies, get their names and spiritual rank, but little would be accomplished if the garbage was still there. You may be able to chase them off, but they would just find seven others and tell them where the garbage is (see Luke 11:26). The answer in this church age is repentance and faith in God.

The gospels clearly showed the supremacy of Christ over the kingdom of darkness. Everything changes under the New Covenant. The responsibility has shifted from an outside agent to the individual. We can't put on the armor of God for other people. We can't repent and believe for them, but we can help them. The apostle Paul explains how to do that in 2 Timothy 2:24–26 (NASB):

> *The Lord's bond-servant must not be quarrelsome, but be kind to all, able to teach, patient when wronged, with gentleness correcting those who are in opposition, if perhaps God may grant them repentance leading to the knowledge of the truth, and they may come to their senses and escape from the snare of the devil, having been held captive by him to do his will.*

The passage reads like a truth encounter, rather than a power encounter. Truth sets people free and Jesus is the truth. God is the One who grants repentance. The Holy Spirit will lead them into all truth, and that is the truth that will set them free. Our role is to be dependent upon Him, avoid quarreling, be kind, and patiently speak the truth in love. That was the truth I was looking for, but I still needed to understand the battle for their minds and to learn how prayer fits in.

At the seminary a colleague was looking around to make sure nobody would hear, and then whispered to me, "Are you a charismatic?" I said, "What I am teaching has nothing to do with that controversy. The spiritual battle between good and evil is a major theme of the Bible and therefore needs to be addressed. Spiritual warfare is not a side issue, and it is not the only issue. It is part of our present-day reality." Another colleague asked, "Have you cast any demons out of anyone today?" I said, "I don't do that." He looked rather puzzled and walked off without saying another word. These two men were my friends, but it revealed all the stereotypes that I had to live with. I knew that I could move no faster than I could educate, but the only ones interested at the time were students.

Our natural present-day reality is transient as the apostle Paul said, "For this light momentary affliction is preparing for us an eternal weight of glory beyond all comparison, as we look not to the things that are seen but to the things that are unseen. For the things that are seen are transient, but the things that are unseen are eternal" (2 Corinthians 4:17–18 ESV). It is hard for western rationalists to wrap their minds around the truth that the spiritual world is as real as the one we can see with our natural senses. Yet rationalists do believe in radio waves that surround them, and they make use of them every day even though they are not discernable through their five senses. The Bible teaches, "For we do not wrestle against flesh and blood, but against rulers, against the authorities, against cosmic powers over this present darkness, against the spiritual forces of evil in the heavenly places" (Ephesians 6:12 ESV). The "heavenlies", or "heavenly places", is the spiritual realm that eternally exists all around us. The evidence is all around us, but the world explains it away, as do the worldly in the church.

One of my students said, "Do you mean to tell me that there are demons in this room or on this Christian campus?" I said, "I'm pretty sure there are, but so what? God is here." I went on to explain that there were also germs present in the room. Since everybody believes that, what should we do? Should we start looking for them? You will end up being a hypochondriac if you do. The proper response is to live a balanced life and your immune system will protect you. There are demons all over this world. So live a righteous life. Christ is your immune system. When you put on the armor of God, you are putting on Christ. No church building is a sanctuary. Our only sanctuary is our position in Christ.

Then he asked, "If it is that simple, then why do we even have to know about them?" I answered, "For the same reason we need to know about germs." Two hundred years ago we didn't know germs even existed. Consequently doctors didn't scrub up before surgeries, and they didn't sterilize their instruments. People died. If we believed that there was no spiritual opposition, people wouldn't put on the armor of God, nor would they know enough to take every thought captive to the obedience of Christ. Satan is not our focus, but he must not be ignored. The apostle John wrote, "We know that we are from God, and the whole world lies in the power of the evil one" (1 John 5:19 ESV).

How does the whole world lie in the power of the evil one? Satan, being the father of lies, is "the deceiver of the whole world" (Revelation 12:9 ESV). People are in bondage to the lies they believe. "Beloved, we are God's children now" (1 John 3:2 ESV), but consider who we formerly were and the spiritual environment in which we presently live according to Ephesians 2:1–3 ESV:

> *And you were dead in the trespasses and sins in which you once walked, following the course of this world, following the prince of the power of the air [Satan], the spirit that is now at work in the sons of disobedience – among whom we all once lived in the passions of our flesh, carrying out the desires of the body and the mind, and were by nature children of wrath, like the rest of mankind.*

Immorality is the primary consequence of this mega-deception, but fear is what paralyzes us. Fear is the primary reason Christians don't share their faith, and why they don't want to talk about death and the devil. Many have asked me, "Aren't you afraid to deal with these issues?" There is not a verse in the Bible that teaches us to fear Satan, in fact, quite the opposite. Just like I had to help my visitation evangelism students get over the fear of witnessing, I had to help the Christian community get over the fear of Satan.[9]

How prevalent is the problem of fear? It is the first emotion expressed by Adam after he sinned. "Fear not" is the most repeated commandment in Scripture, occurring 400 times. Anxiety disorders are the number one mental health problem in the world. Most Christians have a greater fear of Satan than they do of God. If we elevate Satan as a greater object of fear, we elevate him as a greater object of worship.

Fear is a God-given emotion. Any time our physical or psychological safety is threatened, fear is the natural response.

9 Anxiety disorders include fear, anxiety, and panic attacks. Rich Miller and I wrote *Freedom From Fear* (Harvest House), to help the church overcome such disorders.

Fear must have an object and we categorize fears by their object. Claustrophobia is a fear of enclosed places, agoraphobia literally means a fear of the marketplace, arachnophobia is the fear of spiders, and so on. In order for a fear object to be legitimate it must have two attributes. It must be seen as imminent (present) and potent (powerful). The major fear objects are death, man, and Satan.

Rattlesnakes are a legitimate fear object for me. But at this moment, while writing, I have no fear of them, because there are none here. They are still potent, but not imminent. All you have to do is remove one of the attributes, and the object is no longer feared. Physical death is still imminent, but it is no longer potent. The apostle Paul wrote, "O death, where is your sting" (1 Corinthians 15:55 ESV), and "For to me to live is Christ, and to die is gain" (Philippians 1:21 ESV). Christians have eternal life and shouldn't fear physical death. The ones who don't have that fear are free to live today.

Jesus said, "And do not fear those who kill the body but cannot kill the soul. Rather fear Him who can destroy both soul and body in hell" (Matthew 10:28 ESV). Another person could take my physical life, but not my soul. I would just be absent from my body and present with the Lord in a resurrected body, which is much better. "Now who is there to harm you if you are zealous for what is good? But even if you should suffer for righteousness' sake, you will be blessed. Have no fear of them, nor be troubled" (1 Peter 3:13–14 ESV).

Satan, like death and people, is also imminent. Therefore, "Be sober minded; be watchful. Your adversary the devil prowls around like a roaring lion, seeking someone to devour" (1 Peter 5:8 ESV). Satan and his hoard of demons are imminent in this fallen world, but no longer potent. The Lord disarmed the enemy. To illustrate, consider two children playing in the kitchen when a wasp starts buzzing around them. They go screaming to their father, who reaches out his hand to grab the wasp. The stinger goes into their father's hand, and then he releases the wasp. The children begin screaming again until the father says, "Children, the wasp has no stinger. It is in my hand." To all those who fear Satan, God our Father is saying look at my Son's feet, His side, and hands.

Why is the fear of God the beginning of wisdom? What two attributes does He have that make Him the ultimate fear object? God is omnipresent and omnipotent. He is the singular fear object that displaces all others. "Do not call conspiracy all that this people calls conspiracy, and do not fear what they fear, nor be in dread. But the Lord of hosts, him you shall honor as holy. Let him be your fear, and let him be your dread. And He will become a sanctuary…" (Isaiah 8:12–13 ESV).

10

Paradigm Shifts

A missionary couple had adopted a young girl from a South American country, and they brought her to the States to attend Biola University. She became a major disciplinary problem, and managed to seduce five Christian girls. The Dean of Students had to confront her and she asked me to sit in on the interview. When the girl left her office the Dean said, "Well, what do you think?" I said, "Are you prepared to accept the fact that not one thing that girl said to you is true?" The Dean was surprised at my response but she did believe me, and in this case I was right.

The Dean of Students referred one of this girl's victims to me and a female professor from Rosemead Graduate School of Psychology (Rosemead). I asked the young woman if she had any mental peace. She started to shake and we both sensed the oppression. I took authority over the evil spirit, and ministered to the young lady. Resolution didn't take long and she left with a peaceful countenance. The professor said, "We have to talk." We both went into my office, she closed the door and said, "Rosemead doesn't know this!" I asked, "Do you?" She said, "Yes, I have had some experience in our church." I asked her why she didn't share what she knew with her colleagues at Rosemead. She said, "I won't do that." So much for academic freedom! She finished her year at Biola and left for private practice.

I have sometimes wondered why a left-brained aerospace engineer felt led to explore the spiritual realm. I was so left-brained at one time that my head tilted to one side! The lure of knowledge and power has never attracted me and I certainly was not following some popular movement. If there was any trend at the time, it was toward psychology and away from the supernatural, at least in evangelical schools. The subject of Satan and demons was considered archaic, medieval, almost barbaric by some. Even among conservative Bible teachers, the subject was acknowledged but not embraced. To this day I don't know my astrological sign, but on the other hand I have never denied the reality of the spiritual world. However, I just had this sense that something was missing. The Bible seemed to offer more hope and victory than what I was seeing in our churches.

My first experience on campus as a professor was during orientation for new teaching staff. A pleasant young lady was introduced as an assistant professor in psychology by the President, who then said, "And by the way, she is also our youngest Christian. She found the Lord just last year." I could hardly believe what I was hearing. I got to know her later and she was a terrific person, but how could she possibly have had the time to integrate her new-found faith with her secular psychology education?

It wasn't just at our school where this was happening. All across the country Bible colleges and seminaries were adding psychology degrees classroom. In order to be accredited, the faculty should have research doctorates, but there were no Christian schools offering such degrees at that time. There is just a handful today, and all their teaching staff have secular degrees. Some of the more fundamental schools stood against this trend, and for good reason. But when I listened to their rhetoric and that of the religious far right I couldn't identify with them either. Their anti-psychology message was often coupled with legalism and many were against anything that got too personal. Besides, psychology, by definition, is a study of the soul, and I was not against that. In fact I believed a truly biblical psychology was sorely needed.

It seemed like I didn't fit anywhere. I didn't want to be like those who pounded the Bible the hardest, even though I deeply believed the Bible to be God's inspired word. I didn't feel comfortable with psychology professors, even though they seemed to be nicer than the legalists. I had good friends on the seminary faculty, but they weren't much interested in what I was pursuing, which was a comprehensive answer for people's problems. During those first five years I underwent three major paradigm shifts affecting how I did ministry, which would have had the potential to separate me even further from the status quo. However, I was not going to let that happen on a relational level. I am a bridge builder by nature, and I would not take any steps forward that might be divisive or cause the loss of fellowship.

If one has the goal of learning how to solve people's problems, then where you start from matters. Given my seminary education, I had no choice. I started with a theological foundation, and the authority of God's word was the grid by which I evaluated any data. From that foundation I gleaned my psychology from the Bible with a biblical worldview that included the reality of the spiritual world.

Understanding the spiritual battle for our minds was the

first paradigm shift. In the process of trying to understand how people develop their worldview I was studying 2 Corinthians 10:3–5 (ESV):

> *For though we walk in the flesh, we are not waging war according to the flesh. For the weapons of our warfare are not of the flesh but have divine power to destroy strongholds. We destroy arguments and every lofty opinion raised against the knowledge of God, and take every thought captive to obey Christ.*

This passage is not talking about defensive armor. It describes a divinely inspired offensive attack against thoughts raised up against the knowledge of God. Where did those thoughts come from? Let me explain. We are born into this world physically alive, but spiritually dead. During those early and informative years we have neither the presence of God in our lives, nor do we have a knowledge of His ways. So we all learn to live our lives independently of God. Our worldview, values, and attitudes are assimilated from the environment in which we are raised. Strongholds are flesh patterns, which are mental habit patterns of thought. They are similar in concept to what psychologists call defense mechanisms.

Then one day we are born again, and we are new creations in Christ. "The old has passed away; behold, the new has come" (2 Corinthians 5:17 ESV). We have been delivered from the domain of darkness and transferred to the kingdom of God (see Colossians 1:13 ESV). We are no longer "in the flesh," we are alive in Christ (Romans 8:9 ESV). That is gloriously true, but an honest new believer may think, *If that is true how come I still feel the same way, and struggle with the same old issues?* That is the experience of every new convert, because everything that was programmed into their mind in the past is still there. That is why the apostle Paul wrote, "Do not conform any longer to the pattern of this world, but be transformed by the renewing of your mind" (Romans 12:2). We can continue conforming to this world, but we are urged not to do so. This transformation will take time, because there is no way to instantly renew our minds.

There is a fundamental difference between our brains and our minds. Our brains are physical matter and part of our bodies, but our minds are part of our souls. This brain/mind combination is analogous to a computer operation that has two distinct components, namely the software and the hardware. The brain would be the hardware, and the mind would be the software. Of course one can have a hardware (neurological) problem, but the primary focus of Scripture is on the software, that is, the mind. Making this distinction has major implications for the use of medications that may be necessary for physical illnesses. Taking a pill to cure your body is commendable, but taking a pill to cure your soul is deplorable.

It sounds simple, but if Christians want to grow (be transformed) they need to reprogram their computers (minds), but they'd better check for viruses. We are not just up against the world – the world system we were raised in – and we are not just struggling with flesh patterns. The enemies of our sanctification are the world, the flesh, and the devil. Computer viruses are not accidental. They have been maliciously introduced to destroy the system, and that is precisely what Satan wants to do.

The apostle Paul wrote, "The Spirit clearly says that in later times some will abandon the faith and follow deceiving spirits and things taught by demons" (1 Timothy 4:1). That is presently happening all over the world. I have personally worked with hundreds of people who are struggling with condemning, blasphemous thoughts, and hearing voices that are contrary to God's word. These "voices" can be singular or multiple, and they take on distinctive personalities. In almost every case it has proven to be a spiritual battle for their mind, and I have learned how to help them resolve their personal and spiritual conflicts through genuine repentance and faith in God. Most discover for the first time the peace of God that is now guarding their hearts and minds "in Christ Jesus" (Philippians 4:7).

It is easy to understand why people are reluctant to share such thoughts – and most won't if they suspect you don't believe them. I am not the only one who is dealing with this mental battle. Every psychiatrist and professional counselor is working with people who are struggling mentally. They just have a different explanation for it. Chemical imbalance is the most common explanation. But how could a chemical produce a thought or a personality? And how could our neurotransmitters randomly create a thought that we are opposed to thinking? Is there a natural explanation for that? The likely explanation you would hear from the secular world, and from Christians who have been secularly trained is: "They were given an antipsychotic medication and the voices stopped." Sure they stopped, and so did almost everything else! Remove the medication and the thoughts or voices are back, so nothing is really resolved. They just narcotized it. Which is the same reason why people drink and take drugs. They have no mental peace so they drown out the thoughts with alcohol and drugs, only to wake up the next morning a little bit worse.

The apostle Paul instructed the Corinthians to "take every thought [*noema*] captive to obey Christ" (2 Corinthians 10:5 ESV).

The Greek word *noema* occurs in Scripture about six times, five of which are in this epistle. The other four are as follows – notice the spiritual context for each occurence:

> *Paul has urged the church to forgive an offender "so that we would not be outwitted by Satan; for we are not ignorant of his designs [noema]."*
>
> 2 Corinthians 2:11 ESV

> *"But their minds [noema] were hardened. For to this day, when they read the old covenant, that same veil remains unlifted, because only through Christ is it taken away."*
>
> 2 Corinthians 3:14 ESV

> *"Even if our gospel is veiled, it is veiled only to those who are perishing. In their case the god of this world has blinded the minds [noema] of the unbelievers."*
>
> 2 Corinthians 4:3–4 ESV

> *"But I am afraid that as the serpent deceived Eve by his cunning, your thoughts [noema] will be led astray from a sincere and pure devotion to Christ"*
>
> 2 Corinthians 11:3 ESV

A faculty wife was ill with cancer, and her husband called on her behalf. She was fearful and wanted to see me. So I went to their home. Earlier, I had given her the bookmark with the "The Believer's Identity in Christ" passages. She said, "I want you to know that list has held me together these past few months." Then, to my surprise, she said, "Neil, I'm not sure I'm a Christian." She was a lovely

Christian woman, so I asked her why she would even think that way? She said, "When I go to church I have these blasphemous and evil thoughts." I said, "Those are not your thoughts. Did you make a conscious choice to think those thoughts? Did you want to think those thoughts?" "No," she answered emphatically. With her maturity it only took a half hour to free her from that oppression. If those thoughts had been representative of her basic nature, then she would have been correct in questioning her salvation, but they weren't. From that time on she never questioned her salvation again, and the fear was gone because she no longer feared death.

How many prisoners incarcerated for a crime they committed are hearing voices? All of them, and they will probably tell you they are, but people in your church won't. If you attend a recovery ministry you will hear people say, "Don't pay attention to that committee in your head," or "You have to get rid of that stinking thinking." I'll have more to say about this battle for our minds later in the book.

The second paradigm shift had to do with prayer. God was sending people to see me with all kinds of problems, and I would get stuck. I would say to them, "I don't know how to help you, but I know God does. If you want to stick with me, we'll just search Scripture together until we find the answer." The apostle James wrote, "If any of you lacks wisdom, let him ask God, who gives generously to all without reproach, and it will be given him" (1:5 ESV). With that in mind, I would stop and pray during sessions and ask God for wisdom. Sometimes I would sit silently for several minutes. Occasionally I would sense God's leading, but I started to feel less comfortable doing that. Not that I thought it was wrong, it just didn't seem complete.

During my college ministry years, I had learned to listen

during my prayer time and let God prioritize my prayer list. I discovered how personal God was, because He would always bring to my mind any issues that were affecting my relationship with Him. I had applied this to myself, but not with others. Now in ministry I was asking God for wisdom, thinking He would give me fresh insights about the other person so I could share that with them. Surely, that would make me a medium! The apostle Paul wrote that God "desires all people to be saved and to come to the knowledge of the truth. For there is one God, and there is one mediator between God and men, the man Christ Jesus" (1 Timothy 2:4–5 ESV). Since I am not supposed to function as a medium, I thought, *Instead of me praying for wisdom on their behalf, why don't I have them pray?* My ministry took a 180-degree turn overnight. That simple concept has changed the way I do ministry.

Let me illustrate this principle. Suppose you are a father who has two young boys. The younger brother is always asking his older brother to come to you on his behalf and ask if he can go to the movies that night. If you are a good parent, would you accept that? Can you have a secondhand relationship with one of your children? A good parent would say, "Go find your brother and tell him to come see me himself." Similarly, nobody can do somebody else's praying for them. I believe in intercessory prayer, but God never intended that to replace an individual's responsibility to pray. I would still pray and ask for wisdom, but that would be for me, and not for the other person. If they want God's wisdom, they should pray themselves. Then they should listen and not harden their hearts.

One afternoon I wrote out some simple petitions that the inquirer would pray during a freedom appointment (our name for a counseling session). That was the first rough draft of the "Steps to

Freedom In Christ" (or Steps), which are now being used all over the world. I wasn't sure what would happen the first time I tried this approach. Would the person cooperate, I wondered? Now I take some time to hear a person's story, and then ask, "Would you like to resolve this?" Nobody has ever said "No," to that question. Then I say, "With your permission then, I would like to lead you through these steps to freedom," and hand them a copy of the Steps. I explain the process and say, "What's going to happen here today is not what I do, but what you do. Let's start by having you pray this prayer in the Steps out loud."

It is not my intention here to reproduce my book, *Discipleship Counseling* (Regal Books, 2003). I only want to show the message of Freedom In Christ and how God prepared me. If you are not familiar with the ministry, then you might be wondering if this really works. Let me fast-forward a few years and share some research results.

Judith King, a Christian therapist, did some pilot studies in 1996. All three of these studies were performed on participants who attended a Living Free in Christ[10] conference and were led through the Steps during the conference. The first study involved 30 participants who took a ten-item questionnaire before completing the Steps. The questionnaire was re-administered three months after their participation. It assessed for levels of depression, anxiety, inner conflict, tormenting thoughts, and addictive behaviors. The second study involved 55 participants and the third had 21 participants. The following table illustrates the *percentage of improvement* for each category.

10 This conference is now available as a small group curriculum, and can be purchased from our Freedom In Christ offices in several languages.

Pilot Study	Depression	Anxiety	Inner Conflict	Tormenting Thoughts	Addictive Behavior
1	64%	58%	63%	82%	52%
2	47%	44%	51%	58%	43%
3	52%	47%	48%	57%	39%

Research was also conducted by a ministry in Tyler, Texas and in Oklahoma. Most people attending a Living Free in Christ conference can work through the repentance process on their own using the Steps. In my experience about 15 percent can't, because of difficulties they have experienced. At Tyler, a personal session was offered them with a trained encourager. They were given a pre-test before a Step session and a post-test three months later with the following results given in *percentage of improvement*:

	Oklahoma City, OK	Tyler, TX
Depression	44%	52%
Anxiety	45%	44%
Fear	48%	49%
Anger	36%	55%
Tormenting Thoughts	51%	27%
Negative Habits	48%	43%
Sense of Self-Worth	52%	40%

In the above studies the encouragers were all lay people. Participants were chosen on the basis of need. Only those who needed the most help were given an individual appointment. Not all had the same problem, which makes the data even more impressive. They were given only one appointment, but it could have lasted several hours.

My third paradigm shift logically followed the second. It was no longer about me trying to help another individual. Now when I meet with someone I do so knowing that three parties are always present. There is a role that God and only God can play in the inquirer's life. I can't set a captive free, and I can't bind up the broken-hearted, which is what Jesus came to do (see Isaiah 61:1; Luke 4:18). Think of the setting as a triangle with God at the top as follows, and ask the question: Who is responsible for what?

God

Encourager **Inquirer**

Have you ever tried to be the conscience of your spouse? Did that work? Have you ever tried to assume another person's responsibility? Did that work? We would have a lot more peace and balance in our ministries, work, and families if we knew clearly who was responsible for what.

Each side of the triangle above represents a relationship. The most important side of the triangle for me is my own relationship with God. First of all that relationship has to be right. My relationship with the inquirer is also very important. Secular counselors have no relationship with God and see no need to help their clients have one either. Their entire focus is on the relationship that exists between them and their clients. They have learned not to be an enabler, or rescuer, or co-dependent, and that can be helpful for us. As a Christian encourager I have also learned how to love and accept inquirers without judgment or prejudice. I try not to usurp God's role. He will convict them of sin, so I don't have to do that. I haven't pointed out someone's sin in many years.

What am I actually trying to accomplish in a freedom appointment? I am trying to reconcile the inquirer with God. Discipleship Counseling is a ministry of reconciliation that removes the barriers to their intimacy with their heavenly Father through genuine repentance and faith. The whole world and all its inhabitants are in this mess because of the fall, and God has only one plan, and that is for people to be reconciled to Him and each other. "Therefore, if anyone is *in Christ*, he is a new creation. The old has passed away; behold, the new has come. All this is from God, who through Christ reconciled us to himself and gave us the ministry of reconciliation; that is, *in Christ* God was reconciling the world to Himself, not counting their trespasses against them, and entrusting to us the message of reconciliation" (2 Corinthians 5:17–19 ESV, emphasis added).

Back on campus I was seeing God set so many free from multiple problems, and word was getting out. I asked the Dean of Rosemead if he would like to cross-list my class with their school and I got an emphatic, "No." I asked him why. He didn't want the class listed on their transcripts because of accreditation, which he was afraid of losing. So the tail wags the dog again! But, he was politically correct. Another dean replaced him, and President Cook instructed him to talk to me about my elective. I wasn't dreading the late afternoon meeting since we were friends, at least were up until them. We had even played golf together a couple of times.

Before our meeting the Dean had gone to the bookstore and purchased my class syllabus. I could tell immediately that he was under duress when he started to point out what he thought were discrepancies. I told him the syllabus was an outline, and he shouldn't draw conclusions about what I am teaching. It was awkward to say the least, which was another indication that I should wait for God's timing and go only where asked.

I left our meeting disappointed and walked into one of the most difficult cases I ever had. She was an undergraduate student, whom I knew from church. I had provided the pre-marital counseling with her and her fiancé at their request. I did sense at the time that she had some control issues, but I didn't know to what degree. (To make matters worse, there was a music group in the chapel above my office and all we could hear were the drums.)

We went to another building after hours, but all the classrooms were locked. So we sat in the hallway and tried to go through the Steps. At the time I didn't know that the young lady had been ritually abused, and she had no mental recall of that either. An undergraduate professor left his office and saw the torment on her face, but wisely walked by. No demon manifested, because I had learned how to make sure that doesn't happen, but it was a struggle. She left that evening with a degree of freedom. On my way home I was thinking, *What if the Dean had just stayed with me a little longer and seen what God can do?*

The next morning the undergraduate professor came to my office. He had seen the young lady the night before, and then again in the morning. He couldn't believe the difference. He had talked to her many times, but never got to the core of her problem. I didn't either. I was successful at helping her get rid of the oppression, but I would learn later that she was suffering from Dissociative Identity Disorder (DID), which cannot be resolved in one session.

Rosemead offered a two-day recovery conference on campus and someone "goofed" and invited me to present a workshop. On the first morning I talked about mental strongholds and the battle for our minds. Two of the workshop leaders attended my presentation, and both asked for help. One sat in front of me and quivered during the entire presentation. During those two days I took those two leaders through the Steps and God set them both free.

One of the presenters was a completed Jew and a licensed professional counselor. Her freedom appointment brought such a change in her that I suggested she go to the restroom, freshen up, and take a good look at herself. She came back to my office with a joyful countenance and said, "I always thought someone else had to pray for me." She is not the only one who believes that.

I don't want to sound like I had a bad relationship with the faculty at Rosemead, because I really didn't. But I was disappointed that they didn't have any interest at the time in what I was learning, even though Dr. Cook wanted that to happen. They did ask me to speak at their chapel the last semester I was at Talbot, and I told them the truth, and they received it. Dr. Clinton Arnold continued teaching the elective after I left and it is now being co-listed and co-taught by Talbot School of Theology, Rosemead Graduate School of Psychology, and the School of Intercultural Studies. That is progress.

The foundation was laid for Discipleship Counseling, but God had one more ministry of darkness in store for me and for my family. This time it was much more intense and life changing.

11

Brokenness

I had no idea what God had in store for me as I left engineering to go into ministry. Maybe someday I would get to be the captain of the gospel ship. I would sail off into eternity with the family of God. We would throw out a few life preservers and save a few folks who were sinking into the watery abyss. We would have some classes and potlucks along the way. You gotta love those potlucks! We would learn to love each other and the One who powered and guided our ship through the storms of life.

However the journey I imagined was to take an unexpected course, and one day a storm of unusual strength engulfed our ship. As we were being tossed around on the angry seas I noticed a dark ship sailing alongside ours. On board that ship were people struggling with incest, rape, fear, anxiety, depression, anger, and all types of addictions. Slowly it dawned on me that I was on the wrong ship. The other ship was the one that I was called to serve on, and not to be the captain. God is the Captain. So I changed ships to serve the Master of my soul who came to set captives free and bind up the broken-hearted. God's ministry of darkness is what brought about this transition in our lives.

Five years after Joanne's surgery to remove cataracts in both her eyes, her doctor suggested that she should have lens implants. So much scientific progress had been made that implanting a lens had become a simple outpatient surgery. At first Joanne was reluctant, and our insurance provider wouldn't pay, calling the surgery cosmetic, but they finally came around. Joanne's doctor and I thought it was the best thing to do.

The surgery was successful, but Joanne emerged from the anesthesia in a phobic state. She had been anesthetized in other surgeries so I couldn't understand why she was so fearful now. I could understand her apprehension before the operation, because having surgery on one's eyeball is not something you look forward to. Just the thought of it can send shivers down your spine, and her emotional state before surgery had been somewhat troubled. Could the anesthetic itself have caused her emotional state? Or could the nature of her post-operative care have been a factor? The cost of medical care had pushed many hospitals into day surgeries that left little time for rest or recovery after such a traumatic experience.

The nurses had to ask for my assistance in helping Joanne come out of the anesthetic. Joanne was just one of several patients that day, and they needed the bed for others who were cycling through the system. People need more emotional care than that. If she had been allowed to spend a night in the hospital, she might have recovered a lot better. Bringing Joanne home that afternoon was an ordeal for both of us. She just couldn't stabilize emotionally, and she now believes she was over-medicated.

The possibility of this also being a spiritual battle became evident the next day. Joanne believed that she had a foreign object in her eye that had to come out. This made no rational sense to me since the surgery had been successful and she could see with nearly 20/20 vision. At that time I didn't understand the battle for our minds, as I do today. For instance, I have seen such deceptive thoughts in young women struggling with eating disorders. The apostle Paul said, "I find then the principle that evil is present in me, the one who wants to do good" (Romans 7:21 NASB). They believe they have evil present in them and they have to get it out. That is the lie behind their purging, defecating, and cutting themselves: But the evil is not their blood, feces, or food. Joanne didn't have an eating disorder, but the deception was similar and it came at a very vulnerable moment.

It is painful to recall this, because much of what followed might have been avoided. Joanne's struggle with anxiety led to sleeplessness and finally depression. For months she never got more than one or two hours of sleep a night. She went from her eye doctor to her primary care doctor to her gynecologist – and finally to a psychiatrist. Since they could not find anything physically wrong with Joanne they assumed she was a head case or a hormone case. They tried hormones, anti-depressants, and sleeping pills, but nothing seemed to work. She lost her appetite and her weight dropped significantly. She was hospitalized five times. By this time our insurance had run out. We sold our house to pay the medical bills and credit card debt, and rented a house that functioned like a duplex. The owners lived in a separate part of the house.

During this time God was giving me a crash course on what was available in our society for people who had problems like Joanne's. It was disillusioning to say the least. Her primary care doctor asked a psychiatrist to stop by Joanne's bed during one of her hospitalizations. Without asking us, he talked to her for fifteen minutes and sent us a bill for $275. When I got the bill I called their office thinking it was a mistake. That was the first I'd heard that he had even visited Joanne. I told the secretary that we didn't ask for the consultation and shouldn't have to pay the bill. I was told that they would turn the bill over to a collection agency if we didn't pay it. So I paid it.

A counselor that Joanne was seeing wanted to have a consultation with me. I didn't want to go, because it meant another $60 that we couldn't afford. However, for Joanne's sake I went. Counselors should hear the other side of the story, so I didn't have a problem with that. I asked her what other husbands do in my case, and she said, "They leave." Then she proceeded to tell me about her dysfunctional marriage, and started to come on to me. That was the last time either of us saw her.

The best support came from Dr. Nick Kurtanic who occupied the office next to mine. Years earlier, Nick had had surgery for cancer and had been three weeks away from death, and he believed that God healed him from melanoma. Nick would wander into my office once or twice a week and ask, "Any change with Joanne?" When I said there wasn't, He'd say, "Let's pray," and we did. I can't tell you how much that meant to me. I just needed someone to stand with me, and Nick was there.

Joanne couldn't function normally for months. My daughter, Heidi, wasn't sure if she could handle it if her mother were to die. So she had a tendency to stay away. My son, Karl, withdrew into himself. He had made the varsity soccer team, starting at left wing, when he was only in the 9th grade. He was a natural athlete, but that was his last year playing competitive sports. He and his mother were very close, and Karl would be the last to recover from this difficult time.

I was caught in a role conflict. Was I Joanne's pastor, counselor, discipler, or was I only supposed to be her husband? I decided there was only one role I could fulfill in her life, one that nobody else could, and that was to be her husband. If someone was going to fix my wife, it would have to be someone other than me. My role was to hold her everyday and say, "Joanne, this too will pass." I was thinking it would be a matter of weeks, but it turned into a 15-month trial. God had dropped us into a funnel again and it was getting narrower and narrower.

Meanwhile at the seminary I was invited to be on the "Dean's Advisory Search Committee," which was carefully selected by Dr. Cook. Who was, or wasn't, on the committee, was making a statement. He had made it clear that we were just advising him in the search for a new Dean of the seminary. The final selection would be his. I don't blame him. The seminary was going through a tough transition. We had an extension of the seminary in a large church at the other end of the Los Angeles basin. We all knew it was just a matter of time before the pastor would separate himself from Talbot and call the extension his own, which he did. Dr. Cook had appointed a female trustee to the Biola University Board and that was all the reason the pastor needed, since he was against any women being in such positions. He told our extension students that their previous credits would be accepted and invited them to join their seminary at half the tuition cost. I can't blame the extension students for going that direction. They sought accreditation for their new seminary, but it was initially denied for ethical reasons.

Dr. Cook made his selection for the Dean of Talbot. Immediately four faculty members resigned, and went to the new seminary. I had a good relationship with those who left and was sorry to see them go. It was an ideological split. The Pastor had Bob Jones University roots, and was more closely aligned to that brand of fundamentalism than that of Talbot. Talbot was, and is thoroughly evangelical, but the school was moving away from old-time fundamentalism, as was the rest of conservative Protestantism. It was probably best for both schools. Talbot's enrollment dipped for a couple of years, but it recovered and continues to grow to this day. Actually, the seminary went through a renewal and ended up better than it was before. Someone said, "You lost your whole Greek department." I said, "You should see the one we've got," which included Dr. Clinton Arnold, who would later teach the elective I'd started on spiritual warfare. Dr. Arnold was a New Testament professor, but he was also a renowned authority on spiritual warfare. Some on the committee wanted me to be the Dean. Dr. Cook met with me to explore that possibility, but there was no question in my mind. I couldn't put any additional pressure on Joanne. Besides, I had no such ambitions.

What troubled me the most at the time was the theological arrogance that I was seeing in Christian higher education. I was teaching my students that, "the goal of our instruction is love from a pure heart and a good conscience and a sincere faith" (1 Timothy 1:5 NASB). Jesus said, "By this all people will know that you are My disciples, if you have love for one another (John 13:35 ESV). Where was the love? I was seeing an academic pursuit, where the Christian walk is little more than an intellectual exercise. The apostle Paul knew something about being humbled when he wrote, "We know that 'all of us possess knowledge.' This 'knowledge' puffs up, but love builds up" (1 Corinthians 8:1 ESV). You can know theology and be arrogant, but you can't have an intimate knowledge of God and be arrogant.

I didn't know how to help Joanne at that time, and God was showing me some things in my own heart that were not pretty.

It's so easy to judge those who can't perform better. You just want to say, "Come on, try harder." But trying harder is not the answer for those who are under the cloud of despair. "Just say no," doesn't work either for those who are in the bondage of sin. God was knocking me off the high horse of simplistic thinking.

During this time I was doing pulpit supply at Calvary Church of the Palisades situated along the coast of California. The Pacific Palisades community is one the richest in the world. Every week I was asked to candidate for the senior pastor position. One week they actually offered me the position with a salary of $100,000, which seemed like a fortune in those days. That was four times the salary that I was making at the seminary, and it would have solved our financial problems. They said, "We'll take a vote after this morning's service." But I knew that I couldn't accept their invitation.

There was a lot going on in my life at that time. Some of my colleagues were saying to me, "I don't see how you are doing it." I was helping everyone else, but I couldn't help my wife, other than to just be there. I have always been known as "mister fix-it." Even my children would say, "Don't worry, Dad will fix it." But I couldn't fix this. I felt helpless and identified with the "one' calling in Isaiah 21:11–12 (NASB):

> *One keeps calling to me from Seir,*
> *"Watchman, how far gone is the night?*
> *Watchman, how far gone is the night?"*
>
> *The watchman says,*
> *"Morning comes but also night."*

A ministry of hope must be based on the truth that "morning comes." No matter how dark the night, morning comes; and it is usually the darkest before the dawn. In our darkest hour, when I wasn't even sure if Joanne was going to live or die, morning came. Joanne had all but given up on any medical answer, but a doctor in private practice was recommended to her. He immediately took Joanne off the medication that she was on, and prescribed a much more balanced approach to dealing with depression. He also helped with her health in general and that included nutrition.

At the same time we had a day of prayer on campus. I had nothing to do with the program other than to set aside special time for prayer in my own classes. The undergraduate students had a communion service that evening. Since I taught at the graduate level, I normally wouldn't have attended, but work had detained me on campus so I decided to participate. I sat on the gym floor with the undergraduate students and took communion. Nobody in the student body was aware that this was one of the loneliest and darkest times of my life. I was deeply committed to doing God's will, and I was walking as best I could in the light of previous revelation, but I felt incredibly lonely and frustrated. There was nothing I could do to change Joanne or the circumstances.

I can honestly say I never once questioned God, nor felt bitter about my circumstances, and I have Him to thank for sustaining me. The Lord had been preparing my heart and leading me into a ministry that helps struggling Christians. Somehow I knew that the nature of my ministry was related to what my family was going through, but I didn't know what to do about it. Should I abandon what I was doing to help others in order to spare my family? God was blessing my ministry in unprecedented ways, but my family was suffering. God had stripped us of everything we owned. All we had left was each other, and our relationship with God. When God is all you have, you begin to discover that God is all you need.

When we had exhausted all our resources, morning came!

If God has ever spoken to my heart, He did in that communion service. There were no voices or visions. It was just His quiet and gentle way of renewing our minds. It didn't come by way of the worship leader's message, or the testimonies of the students; but it did come in the context of taking communion. The essence of my thought process went something like this, *Neil, there's a price to pay for freedom. It cost My Son His life. Are you willing to pay the price?* I remember thinking, *Dear God if that's the reason, I'm willing, but if it's some stupid thing I'm doing, then I pray that you would tell me*. I left that evening with the inward assurance that it was over. The circumstances hadn't changed, but in my heart I knew that morning had come.

Within a week, Joanne woke up one morning and said, *Neil, I slept last night!* From that point on she knew it was over. Joanne never looked back, and continued on to full and complete recovery. At the same time our ministry took a quantum leap. What was the point of all this? Why did we have to go through such a trial?

There are several reasons why God takes some of His children through His ministry of darkness. First, you learn a lot about yourself during those times. Whatever was left of my old nature that gave simplistic advice such as "Why don't you read your Bible" or "Just work harder" or "Pray more" was stripped away. Most people going through dark times want to do the right thing, but they don't know what the right thing is. The proper response is to realize our limitations and deepen our roots in the eternal, while severing ties with temporal answers and props that don't last.

Second, we learn compassion during God's ministry of darkness. We learn to wait patiently with people, weep with those who weep, and refrain from instructing those who suffer. We learn to support the emotional needs of people who have lost hope. Instruction may come later when it is appropriate. I believed that I was a caring person before, but nothing like I am now, because of God's gracious way of ministering to me. Most of the help we received during Joanne's illness was superficial. Friends offered to take Joanne for a ride, or they would say, "You'll feel better," but I was grateful for any help we got.

Even though Job didn't get the emotional support he needed from his friends during his dark hours, we must keep in mind that the final lot of Job was far better than it was at the beginning. The same happened to us. Within two years God replaced everything we had lost, and this time it was better in terms of home, family, and ministry. Be confident that God will make everything right in the end. It's a rough road to freedom. Every bump is a potential benefit, and every curve is a correction until our ways become His ways.

Third, I didn't have any idea how much my stoic, Scandinavian self-sufficiency was my greatest enemy to my sufficiency in Christ. God brought me to the end of my resources in order that I could discover His. I wasn't any smarter when the dawn came. I was just more dependent upon Him. I no longer had any desire to play god in my own life, much less anyone else's. I just wanted to be an instrument in His hands and be a servant in His kingdom.

We don't hear enough sermons on brokenness these days, or see enough examples. It's the great omission, and that's why we can't fulfill the great commission. In all four gospels, Jesus taught us to deny ourselves, pick up our cross daily, and follow Him. When it was time for the Son of Man to be glorified He said: "Truly, truly, I say to you, unless a grain of wheat falls into the ground and dies, it remains alone; but if it dies, it bears much fruit" (John 12:24 ESV). I don't know any painless way to die to self-rule. I do know that denying self is necessary if we want to fulfill our calling, and it's the best possible thing that could ever happen to us. "For we who live are constantly being delivered over to death for Jesus' sake, so that the life of Jesus also may be manifested in our mortal flesh" (2 Corinthians 4:11 ESV).

Moses was no good for God in Pharaoh's court. God had to strip him of his earthly possessions and positions before he could be an instrument in His hand. Chuck Colson was no good for God in the White House, but he became a powerful force in prison. I had a lot of hard-earned attributes including five degrees, but I wasn't much good for God until I suffered the loss of all things. I can't set a captive free or bind up the broken-hearted, but God can. Every book I have written and every recorded message was after this experience. That was the birth of Freedom In Christ Ministries, which has spread all over the world.

Possibly the greatest sign of spiritual maturity is the ability to postpone rewards. The ultimate test would be to receive nothing in this lifetime, and to look forward to receiving our reward in the life to come. This is how the writer of Hebrews 11:13–14 (NASB) expressed it, "All these died in faith without receiving the promises, but having seen them and having welcomed them from a distance, and having confessed that they were strangers and exiles on this earth. For those who say such things make it clear that they are seeking a country of their own." Farther on, verses 39–40a read, "And all these having gained approval through their faith, did not receive what was promised because God had provided something better for us."

I used to tell my students that God's will for their lives is on the other side of a closed door. Naturally we want to know what it is, but why do we want to know? So we can decide whether or not we want to go through the door? If we want to fulfill our destiny, we have to decide something on this side of the door. If God is God then He has the right to decide what is on the other side of the door for us. If we don't give Him that right, then we are playing god with our own lives, and may miss the incredible adventure He has planned for us.

There is another reason why it is best that we don't know what is on the other side of the door. If I had known beforehand what my family would have to go through to get where we are today, I probably wouldn't have come. But looking back, *I'm glad I came.* God makes everything right in the end. It may not even be in this lifetime, as it wasn't for the heroes of our faith mentioned in Hebrews 11. I believe with all my heart that when this physical life has come to an end for all those who embraced their Heavenly Father as Lord and Savior, they will look back and say that the will of God is good, acceptable, and perfect.

In the middle of our dark time a professor in my department resigned. He had directed our Doctor of Ministry (DMin) program and taught pastoral counseling. My expertise was evangelism, discipleship, leadership, pastoral ministry, Christian education, ethics, and spiritual warfare. The seminary was in a budget crunch and the Dean asked me to be the interim director of the DMin program, and teach pastoral counseling. This represented a career change that I would never have made under normal circumstances, but it proved to be one of the greatest transitions of my life. I would spend the next twenty years writing books that addressed the needs that people have in our churches. I still had so much to learn, and sensed no call to be anything other than the best professor I could be. Little did I know that God was about to show me the dark side of Satanism, and prepare me for a ministry far beyond the walls of Talbot School of Theology.

12

The Dark Side

I received a phone call from a lady who had a strange story and a request for help. She was a backslidden Christian who rented part of her home to a man in his forties named Harry. Harry claimed to have been raised a Satanist, but now he wanted out of it. She wanted to know if I could help him. So I arranged for the three of us to meet at our church on Saturday afternoon. After hearing his story I said, "You can't just leave Satanism, and go nowhere, because you would still be in the kingdom of darkness. Are you prepared to make a decision for Christ, which is your only way out?" Immediately Harry started to shake and I could sense the oppression.

I didn't want to proceed without some prayer support, and his nominal Christian lady friend wouldn't be much help for that. So I asked them to wait while I looked to see who was available. The only other person on location was the custodian, but I knew him to be a strong believer. So I explained the situation and said to him, "You don't have to do anything, just be there to support me in prayer."

Back in my office, I again asked Harry if he would like to make a decision for Christ. When he said, "Yes," all hell broke loose. My custodian friend will never forget that day. If there had been a door at that end of the office where he was praying, he probably would have used it. Fortunately I knew Harry's antics wouldn't bring about the fear response in me the enemy hoped for. I opened my Bible and started reading out loud from the first chapter of Ephesians, which describes our position in Christ. I inserted Harry's name as follows: "Blessed be the God and Father of our Lord Jesus Christ, who has blessed [Harry] in Christ with every spiritual blessing in heavenly places," and so on. I continued through most of the chapter. Within a matter of minutes Harry was still trembling, but was lying prostrate on the floor. With a great deal of effort he managed to slowly say one word at a time, "Lord Jesus, I need you." Instantly he was released and was able to sit up.

That may have been the most humble decision for Christ that I have ever seen. Coming to Christ, however, was just the beginning and not an end. Like every new believer, the flesh patterns were still there – only Harry's flesh patterns were considerably darker than most. Additionally, he had major spiritual opposition, and the mental harassment was intense. Harry also had to deal with Satanists who made threatening calls, and was told in no uncertain terms that he'd better not go public with his testimony. Two Christian men took the time to be with him wherever he went. If I had known then what I know now, I could have helped him a lot more through the repentance process.

I told Harry that my students had asked me about signs and symbols of Satanism, and I asked him if he could share with me what he knew. The next time we met he showed me a page of symbols. Another page had seals identifying the seven major covens of the world. Two of the seven seals were designated for eastern and western United States. I'd been expecting to see pentagrams and goat heads, and so on, but this was completely different, which raised a question. What should I do with these two pages? The answer was nothing. I had no idea if it was true or not, and there was no way to verify it one way or another. However, I did see the seal designated for the western United States etched into the skin of three other individuals over the next two years.

Harry did share one valid point that I believed. He said, "What you see is not what you need to be concerned about. Public figures who call themselves Satanists, like Anton LeVey, are not the real thing." LeVey was demonized for sure and therefore evil, but not a true Satanist. Sometime later, Harry's lady friend called to say that he had made a deal with the Satanists. They promised not to harass him any more if he kept his mouth shut. They had previously broken into his home, and hog-tied and branded him. That was the last I heard of Harry. You don't make deals with the devil or his minions.

A local television station had a Sunday afternoon program that dealt with a variety of issues. They called and asked if I would be a guest on their show. A policeman and counselor would be joining me, but the special guest was a lady flown in from another state who claimed she was raised in a Satanist home. She had fled for her life when she was about 19 years old, and never contacted her parents or relatives again. Now in her late fifties she was there to tell her story.

I was relieved to find out that the counselor was a Christian who had some experience working with those who had been ritually abused. The policeman was the Los Angeles, California "expert" on Satanism, assigned to work on occult crimes, but he was on a different page than the counselor and myself. He dealt with dabblers who paint swastikas on gravestones and drug dealers who claim to be Satanists. These are dangerous people for sure, but not hard-core underground Satanists who belong to a strictly secret society. The policeman started out a little cocky, but was smart enough to realize that his knowledge was superficial. The guest speaker was not a Christian, but was relieved that the counselor and I not only believed her story, but also were able to validate her experiences, which isn't always the case.

After the show I asked her what she was doing to protect herself, and learned that she sprinkled salt around her house and did other rituals. I told her that if she were to become a Christian she would have all the protection she needs in Christ, and have the support of the Christian community. Unfortunately her escorts whisked her away before she could respond, and I never saw her again.

On another occasion I was counseling two ritual abuse victims when Friday the 13th happened to coincide with a full moon. I had no prior knowledge of the spiritual significance of such occurrences, but both inquirers called me that week and complained of more than the usual spiritual harassment. A month later two policemen stopped by my office after their pastor, a former student of mine, had suggested they talk to me. During the week prior to that Friday the 13th a 19-year-old woman had walked into their police station and said that she feared for her life. She claimed that her parents were Satanists and she believed that she was going to be sacrificed that Friday evening. Fortunately the woman behind the desk was a Christian, and a friend of these two officers whom she called for assistance.

They didn't know whether to believe her or not, but chose to err on the side of safety. The female officer went undercover with the young lady to the Friday evening ritual, with the two other officers standing by. Pandemonium broke out and she called for backup. They actually caught the girl's father and uncle engaged in chargeable occult crimes, and arrested them. The female officer took a leave of absence just to be with the young lady who still feared for her life. The two policemen asked me what I thought about their experience.

I cautioned them on two points. First, people like that are going to divulge a lot of information about the dark side. Listen to them, but don't believe much of what they say. Such people are coming out of spiritual darkness where lies are the norm. Some of what they say may be true, but there will be no way to prove it. You have to accept what they say in order to help them, because that is their perceived reality. I advise everyone not to take that information beyond the freedom appointment, unless there is hard evidence to support what they are saying.

Second, it is highly unlikely that such cases will ever get to trial. Satanists won't let it go that far. With a surprised look the policemen said, "You're right. The uncle committed suicide in his cell and her father had pleaded guilty on the grounds of insanity." That was the only case I know of where Satanists were actually caught in the middle of their ritualistic sacrifices. Usually satanic ritual abuse (SRA) victims come for help years after the crime, and most are suffering from Dissociative Identity Disorder (DID), which used to be called Multiple Personality Disorder.

God was giving me a crash course on the kingdom of darkness, which was sorely needed since I had no idea what I was getting into. Nor did I have significant experience with Dissociative Identity Disorder, so I was ill-prepared for my first exposure to it. That happened when a middle-aged lady in my office suddenly looked at me and said, "Who are you? Where am I? I'm getting out of here," and she left. That freaked me out! I had been startled by demonic interruptions, but never frightened by them. This was different, and I asked myself, "What was that?" The next day the lady called and said, "I think I was in your office yesterday. What happened after that?" I wondered the same thing!

I had never seen someone switch personalities right in front of me before. It is an incredible experience. Everything about the person changes. It appears that two or more totally different people are sharing the same body. The personalities may or may not be co-conscious of each other. With one exception, every SRA victim that I have dealt with had DID. Not only was this exception unique, she was the most pitiful person I have ever met. A secular psychologist's diagnosis would likely be schizoid-affect disorder: she was plagued by voices and had zero ability to show any emotion. She couldn't cry, or laugh, or even smile.

I believe God created us with the ability to dissociate. SRA victims have been subjected to such extreme cruelty that they dissociate in order to survive. That allows the person to have a relatively normal development, but like any other defense mechanism it breaks down as they mature. Most will start to recall memories later on in life, which I think reflects the graciousness of God. He waits until they have enough maturity and support before He reveals their past experiences. Even then it will be traumatic, but they are in a better position to deal with the abuse. I call it the "onion effect". Rather than reveal all their past at one time, God peels off one layer at a time. He will probably not reveal the hidden things if we are not responsible for what we already know.

The most informative experience was with a couple I met in

a church. It was one of my first conferences on Resolving Personal and Spiritual Conflicts. They attended the worship time, and then listened to every word I said in another room. The next week they called and asked to see me. They shared an incredible story! Her parents had given her up to be raised by a wealthy man who was her ward. She went to a Catholic parochial school and was expected to get perfect grades. At her ward's instigation she stole chalices and crucifixes from the church that he used in Satanic rituals in the basement of his mansion. Three times she was bred to a young man, and became pregnant. The fetuses were sacrificed.

Near the end of her senior year of high school she came back to the mansion after school as she normally would, but this time federal agents surrounded it. She was questioned for a month, and finally released. Her ward, who she never saw again, had connections to Washington, D.C. and financial power over many holdings. Remarkably, she eventually graduated from college with perfect grades, and pursued her real talent, which was singing. She was near forty when she strolled into a small store where a sweet Christian saleswoman invited her to church. That was the beginning of a long and painful recovery. After receiving Christ she started having flashbacks of those early years.

She always wondered what had happened to the boy that she was bred with; to her shock he showed up one day in the same church. Initially she thought he was an infiltrator, so she kept out of his sight. Then one day she stepped out of the shadows and said to him, "Do you remember me?" He didn't at first, but that was enough to trigger his memories. He too had been subjected to Satanism, and his recovery was even more painful. At first he hated her for being the one who would trigger his memories of ritual abuse, but that changed over time and they eventually married.

After hearing their story, I said, "Good grief, what were you thinking when I came to your church?" They said, "You're right on, and the only one we felt safe enough with to share our story." At the time I was frequently being awakened at 3:00 a.m., as were others that I was working with. I asked them, "What is the deal with 3:00 a.m.?" They told me that satanic rituals begin at midnight and continue to 3:00 a.m., which is like prime time for demonic activity. I was being targeted by the enemy, but I wasn't alarmed because I knew that "greater is He who is in [me], than he who is in the world" (1 John 4:4 NASB). If you did nothing about it, the harassment would end at 4:00 a.m.

Over the years I have asked two questions during this particular conference. First, "How many of you have been alertly awakened at a precise time in the morning, like 3:00 a.m.?" At least a third of the people would raise their hands. Second, "How many have awakened to an overwhelming sense of fear? It could have felt like you were half asleep. You may have felt a pressure on your chest or felt that something was grabbing your throat. You tried to do or say something but couldn't." Again, at least a third of the people would raise their hands. That is a spiritual attack, similar to what is described in Job 4:12–17 (ESV):

> *Now a word was brought to me stealthily; my ear received the whisper of it. Amid thoughts from visions of the night, when deep sleep falls on men, dread came upon me, and trembling, which made all my bones shake. A spirit glided past my face; the hair of my flesh stood up. It stood still, but I could not discern its appearance. A form was before my eyes; there was silence, then I heard a voice: "Can mortal man be in the right before God? Can a man be pure before his Maker?"*

Notice the phrase, "a word was brought to me," but it is not a word from the Lord. This was a message from the accuser of the brethren, "who accuses them [us] day and night before our God" (Revelation 12:10 ESV). I experienced the same attack each night before I started a conference, and it continued from 1990 to 1994. At first I would really struggle, until I learned how to deal with it. The natural response is to try to say something, or to do something. Then I recalled, "For the weapons of our warfare are not of the flesh but have divine power to destroy strongholds" (2 Corinthians 10:4 ESV). I was trying to fight with my own strength and resources, which will not work against the powers of darkness. We simply cannot stand against Satan in the flesh. We need divine power. The apostle Paul wrote, "For everyone who calls upon the name of the Lord will be saved" (Romans 10:13 ESV). But initially I couldn't verbally call upon the Lord, and I knew that Satan was under no obligation to obey my thoughts since he doesn't perfectly know them. I believe that is why the apostle Paul wrote, "if you confess with your *mouth* that Jesus is Lord …" (Romans 10:9 ESV, emphasis added).

The order of Scripture is also important. We must first submit to God and then resist the devil (James 4:7). We don't have to say anything with our mouth to submit to God, since He knows the thoughts and intentions of our hearts (Hebrews 4:12). With that understanding I could turn to God in my heart, submit to Him and verbally resist the devil. Turning to God freed me to say, "Jesus," and the attack would stop. I think God allows that for our testing. We can try to resolve our personal and spiritual problems ourselves, or we can submit to God.

I was not looking for these experiences, but God was bringing them to me for a purpose. He showed me the dark side of reality, and I came to a very important conclusion. The kingdom of darkness is part of this fallen world, but it is not the task of the church to take on Satan: Jesus has already disarmed him. We are called to teach and preach the gospel. I also had to decide whether I was called to primarily help those who had been ritually abused, which takes a huge amount of time, or was I supposed to focus more on equipping the church. I chose the latter.

Steve Goss, who was our ministry's United Kingdom director and later our International Director, had to make a similar decision. The Lord led Carolyn Bramhall to seek help from Steve and his wife, Zoe. Carolyn was a SRA victim and had suffered from DID for years. She lived in the States for four years, trying to get help. Steve and Zoe were able to lead her to freedom and continued helping her until all her personalities were integrated. Such victims need additional support as they work themselves back into society. I wrote the foreword to Carolyn's book, *Am I A Good Girl Yet?* (Monarch Books, 2005). She now has her own ministry helping those who have been ritually abused in the United Kingdom.

Getting exposed to these victims helped us to be better prepared to equip the church. My experiences were neither isolated nor uncommon, which I became aware of as I traveled around the country. If 300 Christian leaders attended the advanced portion of my conference, a third of them were involved in trying to help ritual abuse victims. The most important lessons I learned had to do with the battle for our minds. We can't read each other's minds, so we have no idea what people are struggling with unless they tell us. Most people are not likely to do that. Consequently, many struggle alone thinking they are the only ones who have such problems. They will readily share what others have done to them, but remain silent about their mental battles. Some churches will deny these struggles, and provide no instruction to help them. The fact that the situation is so easily resolved is the real tragedy. The primary evangelistic appeal of the early church was to offer freedom from spiritual bondage, and being able to help was a test of orthodoxy.

A professional Christian counselor attended the elective I started at Talbot. At the beginning of the class he said, "I am a professional counselor and I have never seen any evidence of the demonic in fifteen years with my clients. I had been doing some reading on the New Age, and I thought I'd better be prepared for the day when I do have such a client." A month later I got a letter from him saying, "Every one of my clients was being deceived and so was I!" Why didn't he see it before? For the same reason most pastors don't see it in their churches. If counselors are only seeking to understand their clients, explain why they are dysfunctional, and help them cope, they will never experience any opposition. The devil couldn't care less, because nothing is getting resolved. Even a perfect analysis doesn't set anyone free. Opposition only occurs when resolution is taking place. Secular counselors are taught not to impose their values on their clients, and have no idea how problems can be resolved through genuine repentance and faith in God.

Pastors won't see much evidence of demonic activity if all they are doing is teaching and preaching. I didn't see it when I was a pastor either, except for a few extreme situations. Such is the case in most churches in the United States. Only the extreme cases get noticed, and the average person's struggles get overlooked. Dr. Irv Wolf was the Pastor of Family Life in a large Evangelical Free Church where I conducted a conference. The church has since led thousands of people to freedom, and 95 per cent of the freedom appointments have been led by lay people. I asked Irv, "Given what you know today and what you knew ten years ago, what is your take on the churches in the United States?" He said, "The average pastor doesn't have a clue what is going on in the minds of the people." I think he is right. I know that I didn't when I was a pastor.

Demons are like cockroaches; they only come out in the darkness. When the lights come on they scurry for the shadows. Their first strategy is to avoid detection. If their cover is exposed, they will resort to some pretense of power to intimidate those who are trying to help. If encouragers respond in fear, they are operating in the flesh and the demons are safe. Nothing gets resolved. The key is to bring those thoughts out of darkness and into the light. The whole battle is deception, which is why truth sets us free. However, we have not been called to dispel the darkness. We have been called to turn on the light. All the darkness in the world cannot withstand the light of one candle.

What I was searching for in those days was a means by which I never had to lose control in a freedom appointment, that is, I wanted to work only with the inquirer, and not allow demons to manifest. Assuming that I was filled with the Holy Spirit and was exhibiting self-control, how could I help the inquirer maintain self-control? The mind is the control center, so if they don't pay attention to a deceiving spirit, they won't lose control. I learned to put that responsibility back on the inquirer. They are responsible for their own thoughts.

In a freedom appointment I never saw any opposition when I was only hearing their story, because nothing was getting resolved. Then I would ask, "Would you like to resolve this?" When they said, "Yes," (and they always did) I would say:

> *With your permission, I would like to lead you through these "Steps to Freedom In Christ." What is going to happen here today is not what I do, but what you do. Before we start I need to ask for your cooperation on one very important issue. Your mind is the control center of your body. If you don't lose control in your mind, then we won't lose control during this time together. So if you have any thoughts contrary to what we are doing, or thoughts opposing God, just share them with me. As soon as you bring those thoughts out in the light the power is broken. You may not even have any thoughts like that, but I'm asking in advance just in case you do. I don't care if those thoughts are your own, or if they are coming from a speaker on the wall, or if they are coming from the enemy. The only way they can have any effect on you is if you believe those thoughts and act accordingly.*

The most common thoughts are, *"I have to get out of here,"* and *"This isn't going to work."* Whenever they share such thoughts I just say, "Thank you for sharing that. Let's go on. They will be gone when we are done." The most common physical symptoms are headaches and feelings of nausea. When they share that, I respond in a similar fashion. "Thank you for sharing that, those feelings will be gone when we are done," and they always are. Almost every inquirer will sense no mental peace until the last step is finished. Resisting the devil isn't the big issue, submission to God is what we are trying to accomplish. He is the One who grants repentance and leads them into all truth, and that is what sets them free.

On one occasion I could tell that an inquirer was being distracted, and I asked, "What are you hearing now?" She said, "They are laughing at you." My poor feeble efforts were accomplishing nothing, but to make me an object of ridicule! The first time I heard that I was a little intimidated until I realized the strategy. It is like little children behind a fence taunting those who walk by, because they think they are safe. If the person finds a hole in the fence, the kids run for their lives. When I exposed that strategy, the laughter stopped. It reminded me of 1 Peter 3:14–15 (NASB), "Do not fear their intimidation, and do not be troubled, but sanctify Christ as Lord in your hearts..."

Some inquirers have told me that they had never even considered the option of not obeying or believing those thoughts. Others have trouble separating their thoughts from the enemy's thoughts. Taking them through the Steps will help them clarify that. One woman insisted on her husband being present, which I usually don't recommend. But she needed his presence for emotional support. She had been severely abused, and had trouble maintaining control at first. Halfway through she looked up at me and said with a smile on her face, "Do you know what I am hearing now?" It didn't matter what she was hearing; the battle was over. She clearly understood that those were not her thoughts and she didn't have to pay attention to them anymore. Her mind was quiet when the appointment was over.

Some of these mental thoughts are very subtle. I was doing a conference in Australia. A godly theologian shared his struggle afterwards. Every time he looked at men, he inadvertently looked at their crotch. It had been going on since he was in his early twenties. At first I thought he was struggling with homosexuality, but when I probed in that direction he clearly said that was not his problem. He had told a doctor about it, and got a prescription, but he knew that wasn't the answer. For years he had been wondering, *What in the world is wrong with me?* I asked him, "Now what do you believe?" He said, "There is nothing wrong with me. I'm a heterosexual male child of God." I said, "Exactly, and what should you do about it from now on?" "Just don't pay attention to it, and it will eventually subside."

A godly psychologist friend shared a similar experience about a bizarre thought he struggled with. Every time he had a cup of coffee in his hand and was talking to another person he would have this impulsive thought to throw it in their face. He never did, but for three years he had wondered what was wrong with him. I personally have never heard voices like some of the inquirers that I have had the privilege to help. However, when I first started doing public conferences I did have an unusual experience that went on for four years. I would conclude the conference by leading my listeners through the Steps. As I stepped to the podium a very clear thought would come to my mind: "There is a gun pointed at your head." Now I knew if this were from God, I should duck! But it would not instill any confidence in the congregation to see me ducking around trying to avoid invisible bullets! I must admit that the first time that happened I did casually look around, but never again.

Some are reluctant to share their thoughts because they are vulgar. Others are being intimidated. I could tell that was happening to a lady who came to see me with her pastor. I asked her if the voices were intimidating her and she nodded affirmatively. I said, "If you resolve it here, it will be resolved at home as well." She said, "I wish you could prove that to me." That night she called the pastor and said, "Bob, they're not here either!"

Suppose a mother comes home from the hospital with her third child. She is alone at home and the newborn is crying and the other children are acting up. She is exhausted and suddenly she has a thought: *Kill your babies.* Who is she going to share that thought with? Imagine her husband coming home that evening, and she says, "Hi honey, I have had thoughts about killing the kids!" That is not going to happen. Almost every time I have used that illustration in a conference, some mother has come up afterwards and said, "That has been happening to me." Do these mothers kill their babies? The vast majority don't of course, but very rarely some do. A mother in Texas drowned five of her babies, and she knew it was demonic, but the courts didn't. She was found guilty and pleaded insanity due to post-partum depression. The vast majority who don't kill their babies are left feeling guilty for having such thoughts. The church is failing these people who desperately need to know the truth that will set them free.

I was speaking at a camp when the director woke me up at 1:00 a.m., saying, "We need you in the kitchen." Someone had broken into the pantry from the outside. As we walked toward the kitchen I could see two men at one end of a table, but I didn't see the third person until I stepped through the door. He was the assistant cook, and he was holding a butcher knife to his throat. The first words out of his mouth were, "This so-and-so is going to die tonight." What would you do?

I sat down beside him and said, "No he's not." I said to him, "I know you can hear me now. This is just a voice in your head. You can believe it if you want to and continue holding that knife to your throat, or you can choose not to believe it and put the knife down." The assistant cook had a little trouble regaining mental control and finally said, "Is that all it is?" I said, "Well, isn't it? There is no physical force in this room controlling you. You are just paying attention to a deceiving spirit." He put the knife down, and asked, "If I go to bed will you help me tomorrow?" I told him I would, and he reached under his seat and pulled out an even bigger knife and put it on the table. We gave each other a hug, and off he went to bed. The two amateurs at the other end of the table had been trying to cast a demon out of him to no avail.

You don't want a demon to manifest, because that brings glory to Satan. You want the presence of God to manifest. The glory of God is a manifestation of His presence and He does everything "decently and in order" (1 Corinthians 14:40 ESV).

13

Fresh Wind

Joanne and I bought our first house three months before we got married. Since then we have given up three different homes for the sake of ministry. The first time was when I left engineering to go into ministry. The second time was when I left the pastorate to teach at Talbot. The third time was during Joanne's illness. Morning had come to the Anderson family, and a fresh wind was blowing, but we were dead broke again. I didn't have any money for the down payment on a house, and my salary would have to double if I had any hope of qualifying for a loan. Housing in California was just too expensive for this poor seminary professor.

Call me stubborn if you will, but I had not applied for promotion from Assistant Professor to Associate Professor during my first seven years on faculty. Administration wanted me to, but I couldn't without violating my convictions. Our Provost at the time had come to our school from a secular university and brought with him a faculty promotional package that was anything but Christian. To get advancement you had to sell yourself, and the acceptable criteria included promoting no Christian values. It was all about job performance, and personal accomplishments, based on things you did, and not on who you were.

I was teaching my students to do just the opposite, based on Proverbs 25:6–7. We are called to live righteous lives, and not to promote ourselves. I wasn't disrespectful, but I did tell the administration that promotion based on the values of the world had led to the secularization of many Christian institutions. Finally they did change the criteria for advancement, and I was promoted to Associate Professor.

Joanne and I had made a personal commitment to not seek any positions, nor charge for any counseling, and to never let money be the issue by which we made decisions, other than to be good stewards. Our convictions have been tested, but God has always been faithful. To this day I have never gone to do ministry anywhere that I haven't been invited, and I have never advertised my ministry. If the ministry was to expand, it would have to be by word of mouth. There is no better advertisement than a satisfied customer. When someone's life has been substantially changed, other people take notice. Families, churches, and communities are changed for the good one person at a time, and they are corrupted the same way.

My promotion to associate professor included a small salary increase, but not enough to buy one of the 40-year-old tract homes in our immediate community. So Joanne started looking around for a new house in the distant suburbs. In order to find an affordable house, I would have to commute for at least an hour. Joanne was feeling like a new person and applied for a position at Hunt Wesson as a home economist. Our combined salaries would be enough to qualify for one of those distant homes, but not one near the seminary. We found a newly constructed house in Yucaipa, 62 miles from the school, which might be within our reach financially, but we still had no money for down payment.

After five years of seeing God set captives free and bind up the broken-hearted in private freedom appointments, I sensed that I was ready to equip churches. I was still doing some pulpit supply work at the church in Pacific Palisades. Since they seemed to like me, I thought it would be the perfect place to see how a larger audience would respond to my message. I offered to do a conference on five consecutive Sunday evenings, with two sessions each night, and then finish it on the following Saturday. It went extremely well, and a church in Manhattan Beach, California, invited me to come to their church and do the same thing. I needed some help if I was going to continue doing this: God had just the perfect couple in mind.

Joanne and I had developed a friendship with Jerry and Sally Friesen during my time at Granada Heights Friends Church. Jerry had just sold his airport shuttle business, and was looking for a way to serve God. One night I just felt led to tell Joanne, "I'm going over to Jerry and Sally's house to talk to them about helping me." Jerry was a very good businessman, and Sally was the perfect hostess, but neither had any experience working with people the way I did. I shared with them what I was doing and invited them to come with me to Manhattan Beach. I didn't ask for any commitment. I just wanted them to sit in on the conference, and be prayer partners with me if I had any freedom appointments. This conference, which I entitled Resolving Personal and Spiritual Conflicts, would be offered Sunday morning, Sunday evening, and Wednesday evening for two weeks as part of their regular church services, and then conclude on Saturday. By the time we were done,

Jerry and Sally had caught the vision. They wanted every Christian to know who they are in Christ, experience the freedom that Jesus purchased for them on the cross, and live their new life in Christ in the power of the Holy Spirit. Jerry became our first operations officer, opened up one of his buildings for an office, and contacted his lawyer to see about incorporating the ministry.

I drove Jerry out to see the house that Joanne and I were considering. He liked the house, thought it was a good price, and said, "It looks fine to me, but you don't have any money." I didn't, but God does. Shortly thereafter Dr. Richard Anderson asked if I would do the same conference at the church he pastored in Sierra Madre, California. He would later become our board chairman.

Meanwhile, Joanne and I sensed that God wanted us to buy that house, so we made an offer, which was accepted. I asked for a three-month escrow. To accept that condition they wanted $10,000 earnest money up front. I told them I could get $5,000 in a week. They reluctantly agreed, but they wanted the earnest money the following week. To get that much money I needed 500 people to attend the Saturday session of the conference at the Sierra Madre church. There were no pre-registrations so I had no idea how many would come, but 510 people did attend and paid the registration fee of five dollars per person. On Monday they gave me a check for $5,100, and I gave the realtor a check for $5,000 that same afternoon. The deal would have been off if I didn't have the money that day. However, to qualify for the loan, I still needed to come up with a further $20,000 in less than three months.

All this was happening during the beginning weeks of my spring sabbatical. All teaching staff at Biola University are given a sabbatical every seven years, which can be used in one of two ways. I could teach half time for a year and receive a full salary, or I could teach the fall semester and have the spring semester off with a full salary. I chose the latter. During Christmas break Dr. Peter Wagner and John Wimber were hosting a Power Evangelism Symposium at Fuller Seminary in Pasadena, California. Participation was by invitation only. To be invited you had to be teaching something about spiritual warfare on the seminary level. Most in attendance were missiologists and theologians; I was the only one representing pastoral care. We were asked to present a written paper that we would read at the symposium. Each paper received a formal written response, which was followed by questions from the attendees. I wrote my paper on "The Truth Encounter," which was the last paper presented over the course of three days. The editor for *Gospel Light* was present, and went on to publish the papers in a book entitled *Wrestling With Dark Angels*. That would be my first published work.

The mood at the symposium changed after my presentation. Many said, "This is what I came to hear!" John Wimber, the founder of the Vineyard Churches, was the first to respond. He asked, "Does that work?" I assured him that it did. He said, "How many have you tried that with?" I told them that I had helped hundreds of people who had a wide variety of problems. John continued, "Is this approach transferable, and does it last?" I said, "The results are going to last a lot longer if the person being helped is making their own decisions as opposed to someone else making their decisions for them, and truth is always transferable. The process wouldn't be transferable if it were dependent upon some unique spiritual gift or ecclesiastical office."

Dr. Timothy Warner was present at the symposium, and he invited me to teach a Doctor of Ministry class at Trinity Evangelical Divinity School in Deerfield, Illinois. Tim sat through the class, which is extremely rare for directors of such programs. He was in the process of writing a book about spiritual warfare from a "power encounter" perspective and he made some major changes to his manuscript after the class. A few months later he asked if there was room for him in our ministry, which was just being incorporated. We have had the privilege to work together ever since.

In the fall of my sabbatical year the school paid my way to a writer's symposium, which Biola University was hosting. Most teaching staff in higher education are aware of the mantra, "publish or perish," but I had no such interest. There were about 400 participants and I told my colleague, Dr. Gary McIntosh, that I was probably the only one in attendance who didn't want to write a book. Gary has had some fun with that line over the years! He also became a valuable addition to the Practical Theology Department. I had no interest in being the director of the Doctor Of Ministry program, which I had inherited by default when Joanne was sick. So I recommended that Gary should be offered a contract to become the director, and teach evangelism. Since I had taken over the pastoral care classes, I needed to get that load off my back.

A month had passed since the "Power Evangelism Symposium", when the editor from Gospel Light came to my office and asked if they could publish my book. I asked, "What book?" As we talked, I said, "The material that I have created would probably require two books." But Gospel Light Publications was only interested in doing one book with a first-time author like myself. So they offered me a contract to write *Victory Over the Darkness*. A week later the editor from Harvest House Publishers called and asked if I had signed any contracts yet. They were interested in publishing the other book, and they offered me a contract to write *The Bondage Breaker.* Two months into my sabbatical, I had two contracts to write two books – and I had never written a book before. Who would have ever guessed then, that an unknown author's first two books would each sell over a million plus copies in the next few years, be translated into many languages, and launch a worldwide ministry?

Previously I'd had no plans to write a book, but steps had already been taken to record the core message on videotape. Out of nowhere a man offered to tape 28 sessions in five days. He would provide all the equipment, which included three cameras and a crew of four, and do the editing for $7,000. That seemed like a really low price to me, and it was. He lost his job the next week for doing it that cheaply. The plan was to tape Monday through Friday from 8:00 a.m. to 5:00 p.m. I just had to come up with $7,000.

I have never done any fund raising in my life and I didn't relish the idea then. I contacted a friend from the Pacific Palisades church and she offered to host a dessert party at her home and invite some of her friends. I shared my vision, but I couldn't say the punch line. It was an awkward moment. Finally a man said, "I think what he wants to say is, 'Get out your check books and make this happen.'" We collected $7,000. I have never specifically asked for money to this day. I have let people know what our needs are, and God has always supplied.

The Sunday evening before the week of videotaping, my 14-year-old son, Karl, came home depressed. His best friend's brother had committed suicide. They had found his body in the garage with a noose around his neck. He was a junkie and estranged from his family, a terrible tragedy. This was Karl's first brush with death. I knew the family didn't go to church, so I told Karl to call them and offer my services. When they called me and asked me to do the funeral, I said I could be available any evening that week.

On Monday arrangements were made for the funeral, but they scheduled it for Tuesday afternoon at 2:00 p.m. How could I say no? I asked those who were attending the conference if they would be willing to come Tuesday morning at 7:00 a.m. and we would continue taping until 1:00 p.m.

Shortly before noon on that Tuesday the room began to shake. It was an earthquake! Somehow we finished that day, and off I went to do the funeral. By Friday afternoon we had finished taping the 28 sessions. For several in attendance it was a life-changing experience. One in particular happened to be the wife of one of my seminary students. She said, "I want to help you any way that I can." I asked, "Can you type?" She said, "Of course!" She transcribed all 28 tapes, which turned out to be the text for *Victory Over the Darkness* and *The Bondage Breaker*! Serious editing had to be done, but that launched my writing career.

That was April, and escrow was supposed to close on the house the first week in June. So where was the $20,000 going to come from? During the January interterm of that year, I offered my four-unit class on Pastoral Counseling. This was additional work beyond my contract, which provided the extra income that I needed to survive. I used that interterm to do something very different from the traditional seminary experience. Rather than meet in classrooms at the seminary, we met at the Julian Center, located in the hills east of San Diego. My friend Dick Day had purchased this retreat center to offer a unique learning experience. It was a Francis Schaffer L'Abri-type of experience. He didn't use the camp in January, so I worked out an arrangement with him to do the class there. Dick and I held a common belief that learning best takes place in the context of committed relationships, and I wanted to demonstrate that.

Students were offered the opportunity to bring their spouses and children. We would all chip in with chores, have our meals together, and learn in a relational context. I would lecture in the morning. There would be free time after lunch, and small groups from 3:00 to 5:00 p.m. I could take only twenty-four adults. Three were married and had children. So they made up one small group. Three more were married and had no children. They made up another small group. The remaining twelve singles were divided into two groups. My daughter, Heidi, came along to take care of the children when their parents were meeting. Heidi had just finished training to be a nanny and was planning to move out when she found work with a family who needed her services. Actually, the class had such an effect on Heidi that she went back to Biola to work on a degree.

It was the best teaching experience of my life, and the students said it was their best educational experience. Most of the students connected early on, but one fought the system for two and half weeks. He had come with his mountain bike, weight set, and defensive armor. The process wore down his defenses and he started to be a real person. He was the classic professional student who had it all together on the outside. After the class was over he went back to his church in Rolling Hills Estates, a rich coastal community. He was the president of his Sunday School class and he told them, "You don't know me, because I haven't let you know who I really am." He proceeded to share his experience; and the class got a new president and his wife got a new husband. He appealed to the pastor of his church to invite me to come and conduct a conference, which I did.

Once again, I spoke at their Sunday morning, Sunday evening, and Wednesday evening services for two weeks, and finished on the following Saturday. My honorariums for the six services and the $10 registration fee for Saturday came to $10,000. My student's mother came up to me at the end and said, "I heard from my son that you wanted to buy a house, but couldn't afford one. I would like to give you an interest-free loan of $10,000 if that would help. You can pay me back anytime you want or whenever you can." We had our $20,000, but a slight complication arose.

The seller had my $5,000 earnest money, so they let us move in before escrow was closed, which in hindsight is not advisable. Joanne couldn't commute that far for work, so she resigned her job at Hunt Wesson. We had been given preliminary loan approval based on both our salaries. Somehow they found out that Joanne had quit her job, and withdrew loan approval. Joanne had been seeking other employment, but so far nothing had materialized. The secular world doesn't trust God like we do.

Joanne had interviewed for a position at the Braille Institute in Palm Springs as a home economist, but they hadn't made an offer yet, and they were slow in letting us know. After three tense weeks, the offer came through and we were able to close escrow. For the next three years Joanne would teach the blind how to cook and use kitchen appliances. I would endure the 62-mile commute, leaving either at 4:30 a.m. or after 9:00 a.m. to avoid traffic. That way I could make the trip in about an hour. Then I would drive home before 2:30 p.m. or after 7:00 p.m. At any other time it would have taken me at least two hours to make the journey home.

Yucaipa was a small retirement-type city in the foothills of the San Bernardino Mountains. Close by was Arrowhead Springs, the headquarters of Campus Crusade for Christ. My friend from the Pacific Palisades Church was Associate Executive Director for Community Bible Study. They had their annual meeting at

Arrowhead Springs conference center and one year asked me to be their speaker. One of their key leaders was Camilla Seabolt, a connection that would pay interesting ministry dividends in the coming months.

The largest church in town was Yucaipa First Baptist, so we gave it a try. We were led to an age-appropriate Sunday School class whose teacher was Steve Douglas (who later became the President of Campus Crusade for Christ.) The first Sunday we visited, a man was candidating to be the new senior pastor. The candidate and his wife also visited that Sunday School class and she said, "I know you." What an amazing coincidence. She was a Community Bible Study teacher and had attended the yearly meeting that I just spoken at. That couple was voted in that day.

The Sunday school class was a real treat, not only because I got to meet and know Steve Douglas, but because several in the class were missionaries with Mission Aviation Fellowship. Their headquarters was located in nearby Redlands. The real blessing, however, was getting to know Ron and Carole Wormser. Formerly an Evangelical Free Church pastor, Ron had been on the staff of Campus Crusade for Christ. Later he and five others left Campus Crusade staff to form Churches Alive, a consulting ministry equipping churches to do evangelism and discipleship. Unfortunately, that ministry was going through a major crisis, and they were ready to move on.

Joanne and I invited them to our home one Sunday after church to have some pancakes. We talked all afternoon, and I said, "Maybe you should join our ministry and help me write." They were leaving the next day for a week's vacation. As they left their home on Monday morning, Ron said to Carole, "Do you think Neil meant what he said?" They turned around and came back to our home, and we talked some more. I invited them to come with me to a conference in Sonora, California, and observe.

The Resolving Personal and Spiritual Conflicts conference had taken on a different format. I would start by preaching on Sunday morning, and the conference would begin that evening, and run through Thursday evening, and then conclude on Saturday. On Thursday and Friday I would offer Christian leaders an advanced conference on how to set people free. On Monday through Wednesday I would offer individual freedom appointments. Ron and Carole sat in on those sessions as prayer partners.

The first freedom appointment they sat in on was bizarre. The lady had sexual bondages and demonic experiences. In the middle of the session she suddenly shrieked, and it felt like a bolt of lightning went through the room. I looked at Ron and Carole and said, "Is there any question in your minds as to what we are dealing with here?" They both shook their heads from side to side. The next day was just as bizarre. This lady had tried almost every occult experience available. The Steps have a list of common occult and cult experiences, but she just about doubled what was on that page. I have never seen anything like that since. Usually it takes ten to fifteen minutes to complete that step, but this one took two hours. Wednesday was a little more normal, and Ron said to Carole, "When is Neil going to let us do a session?" Carole's initial response was, "Who cares!"

As soon as we returned home, both Ron and Carole had opportunities to take someone through the Steps – with amazing results. They were hooked. Ironically, in the pastorate Ron had disliked counseling, because people would come back again and again with the same unresolved issues. But this was not counseling in the traditional sense: this kind of ministry is an encounter with God. Within a year, Ron and Carole were doing most of the Discipleship Counseling training as we traveled around the country together. Some of the best years of our lives were traveling with Ron and Carole.

The Doctor of Ministry program at Talbot was one of my departmental responsibilities, and I had arranged for some really good Christian leaders to teach these one-week classes. These were men that I would like to learn from as well, so I enrolled in the program myself. Tuition was free, so why not? It did seem a little awkward to be a student in a class the same year I was the director, but nobody seemed to mind. When I had completed the course work, I had only my dissertation left to write. I saw this as a unique opportunity to resource the church. My dissertation was essentially the same content as *The Bondage Breaker*.

The summer preceding the completion of my second doctoral dissertation, Biola University was having its faculty retreat in Palm Springs. I ended up in a small group in which we were to share prayer requests and then pray for one another. I said to the group, "I think God wants me to write something about what I am teaching and doing, but I really don't want to." I wasn't afraid of the spiritual opposition that I might get; I had already learned how to deal with that. However, I didn't want the academic hassle. I was a member of the Evangelical Theological Society, and writing a book on spiritual warfare would be like committing academic suicide. Such subjects were for the fringe element of the church in the United States.

At the time our seminary was going through an accreditation process. A team representing the American Association of Theological Schools was visiting the campus. They represented a wide spectrum of beliefs. The chairman of their team made an appointment with me, since I was the chairman of the Practical

Theology Department. He asked me about the elective that I was teaching, and I shared truthfully about the class and some of the cases that had been totally resolved through genuine repentance and faith in God.

He shot out of my office and went straight to the dean, and said, "Do you know that you have a faculty member who actually believes in demons?" Fortunately, there was a conservative member of their team that came to my defense. He explained that the church in general has always believed in the presence of a personal devil, and that encounters with demonic forces have taken place throughout church history. He saved the day, and the school passed the accreditation process. But that reaction was just a minor preparation for the criticism yet to come. I really had no idea how cruel some in the church can be, and what the price would be for putting anything into print.

14

Moving On

One of my students at the seminary was on staff with Campus Crusade for Christ. After taking my elective on spiritual warfare he asked if I would speak at an outreach at Cal Poly, Pomona. The college was part of the California college system, and since it was a commuter college, very few students resided on campus. Their plan was to circulate a flyer that read, "Come Hear About Demonic Influences in the World Today." The meeting was scheduled for 7:00 on a Wednesday evening. At the time I wasn't interested in speaking to churches about that subject, much less a secular campus. After some persuasion I agreed, but only with two conditions. They had to have permission to use the auditorium and have adequate prayer support.

If students wanted to come, they would have to remain on campus or come back for the meeting. So I wasn't expecting very many to show up. To my surprise the room was packed with over 250 students. I shared some of my stories of people being released from demonic oppression. I closed with a gospel presentation, asked everyone to bow their heads and led them in a sinner's prayer. If they weren't interested, I asked them to respect those who were, and they did. They were given comment cards to respond to the presentation. Twelve made a first-time decision for Christ, and several asked for personal help. I stayed another hour responding to questions. Almost nobody left, and then we had to close the session and dismiss them. Now I had several backslidden Christians surrounding me asking for help.

A few months later we tried it again at Long Beach City College, a two-year community college. They scheduled the time for 11:00 a.m. on a Tuesday, which I didn't think was a very good time. Crusade staff had reserved the largest auditorium on campus and again it was packed. Essentially we had the same response with several making a first-time decision for Christ. Then another outreach was held at Long Beach State University. This time it was scheduled for Monday at noon. Four hundred people showed up to hear about demonic influences. What if the flyer had said, "Come hear about the claims of Christ?" How many would have shown up? Probably four crusade staff, some curious Christians, and ten trapped friends. These students weren't coming to hear me; they had no idea who I was. They wanted to hear about demons! It did reveal where their interests lay, and raised a question. Is the church missing a golden opportunity to share the gospel?

A year later, I was asked again. This time it would be at Cal State, Santa Barbara, on Halloween night. Anyone who lives in Santa Barbara knows that Halloween is a big deal every year that attracts a lot of counterculture people. Streets are roped off to accommodate the crowds. Crusade had originally reserved a room that would seat around 250 people. Two weeks before the event, the largest auditorium on campus became available. It could seat 1,100 students. So they roped off most of the seats from the center to the back. We were all surprised when nearly 900 students showed up, most wearing costumes. Outside, there was a Satanist group wearing robes, chanting, and holding candles. This was exciting! I'm sure most were disappointed to discover it was a Christian outreach, but several did make decisions for Christ.

We tried the outreach one more time at the University of California in Irvine. This time it was organized by an Asian branch of Campus Crusade for Christ. The room was packed with 200 students on a Tuesday evening. Sitting five rows back was a large Caucasian lady in her fifties who looked like she had lived a pretty tough life. I thought she was representing the sociology department, or some other liberal group, but a warm smile said otherwise.

I gave my presentation and opened up the floor for questions. A man in his thirties, stood up and angrily said, "This man has led you all astray. It is all a pack of lies." Suddenly the large lady stood up and faced him saying, "Listen up. I was a witch and a lesbian until Christ struck me down, and I have been different ever since. Everything that man said is true." Then she sat down and everyone else applauded. Five minutes later the man stood up again, and said, "I want to debate you." She stood up and said, "I'll debate you anytime, anywhere." I gave her a big hug and told her she was beautiful.

One day the head of the philosophy department at Cal State, Dominguez Hills, called me. He asked if I would be willing to debate a man from the American Civil Liberties Union on the subject of school prayer. I told him that I didn't have any strong opinions on the matter, only that we should have the freedom to pray. He said that was enough difference and asked me again if I would be willing to come to their campus. Joanne thought I shouldn't go, because I had no experience debating anyone, and those people are pros. I said, "I'm not going there to win a debate, I'm going to share the love of Christ." Joanne didn't want to witness the carnage, and stayed home with the kids, but she did promise to pray for me.

Before the debate, I met my opponent, Dr. Goldberg. I asked him if he was Jewish. He said, "No, and I never fraternize with the enemy before a debate." I said, "Your enemy? How am I your enemy?" He turned and walked away without saying anything. I knew enough about debates to know that the older man sitting directly in front of me in the audience was a plant. He was there to harass me with questions when the public were given the opportunity. So I waved at him. I was surprised to see a full auditorium.

The head of philosophy was to moderate the debate. We were each given ten minutes, then five minutes, and finally three minutes to respond to each other's arguments. Then the audience was invited to ask questions. The heckler started drilling me with questions. The Campus Crusade for Christ meeting had been canceled that night so people could attend the debate. So I had about fifty Christians going after Dr. Goldberg. What I prayed for actually happened. My opponent lost his cool, and his character revealed itself. My task was not to lose my composure and violate the fruit of the Spirit. I was surprised when the moderator asked me to close the debate with some final words. I had the perfect quote from America's first President, George Washington:

> *Let it simply be asked, where is the security for property, for reputation, for life, if the sense of religious obligation desert the oaths which are the instruments of investigation in courts of justice? And let us with caution indulge the supposition that*

> *morality can be maintained without religion. Whatever may be conceded to the influence of refined education on minds of peculiar structure, reason and experience both forbid us to expect, that national morality can prevail in exclusion of religious principle.*

Coffee and cookies were available afterwards, and I stayed to socialize with the folks. Dr. Goldberg left as fast as he could. I learned later that he was the president of the Orange County Atheistic Society. One student said to me, "That was so cool. He got angry and abusive, and you just kept smiling." Thank you Jesus.

Those were exciting experiences, and they broadened my base of understanding this fallen world and its inhabitants, but it was not my calling to be an evangelist or an apologist. My niche was to show how the church can set captives free, and bind up the broken-hearted. We are commissioned to make disciples, not just converts. Conversion is the first step in the ministry of reconciliation, but they need to be firmly rooted "in Christ," and that is going to require genuine repentance and faith in God. People all over the world are coming to Christ, but few are being discipled. They come to church carrying a lot of baggage from the past. They hear a good message, pick up their bags, and go back home the same way they left. Liberal churches refer them to secular counselors, legalistic churches scold them for not behaving better, and most conservative churches offer them programs. Programs don't set people free, and even good preaching, as important as it is, won't connect with those who are torn up on the inside. They need an encounter with God.

I truly loved teaching at Talbot, but outside ministry was

distracting me from my teaching duties. I was facing the most difficult decision of my career. I couldn't be a good professor and continue responding to all the requests that I was getting from churches and individuals. In May of 1991, Dr. Cook asked if I was going to be at the faculty luncheon the following week. I hadn't planned to go, since this was an all-University faculty luncheon, and not mandatory, but he strongly suggested that I attend. So I thought I'd better be there. To my complete surprise I was presented the "Faculty Excellence of the Year" award. That was the best honor that I have ever received, because the entire University faculty – around 150 of my colleagues – voted on it. It was also a very sad moment, because I knew in my heart that next year would be my final year at Talbot.

I have never grieved over a loss before, but I did that year. Faculty contracts are given out annually at the beginning of the spring semester, and I knew God wasn't going to let me sign mine. I had three degrees from Talbot, my children attended Biola University, and the faculty in the Practical Theology Department were more than colleagues, they were good friends, and you don't always have that in ministry. Under the leadership of Dr. Cook, the University had become more grace-oriented, and more conservatively mission-minded. It was comfortable there.

I must say that the school was very accommodating: I was able to teach most of my classes on one or two days of the week. I was gone many weekends, and individual appointments were taking up a lot of my time. Jerry Friesen was setting up our office in La Habra, complete with phones, copiers, and whatever else was needed to support the ministry. Initially we incorporated the ministry just to make material available. We started with two books, and divided the 28-video set into three sets: "Resolving

Personal Conflicts," "Resolving Spiritual Conflicts," and "Helping Others Find Freedom In Christ."

In December 1991, I was teaching a doctor of ministry class at Talbot School of Theology on "Resolving Personal and Spiritual Conflicts." In attendance were Robert and Grace Toews from Canada. Robert had come to support Grace who was taking the class for credit. Both had lost their previous spouses to illness. Robert had worked for years in the public school system, and retired as a superintendent. Grace had been a missionary in Thailand. Neither was affiliated with any ministry at the time, and both had a Christian and Missionary Alliance background. Over lunch one day I asked if they had any interest in representing us in Canada. They were interested, and we stayed in contact with each other.

When I didn't sign my contract that next spring, I knew there was no turning back. Near the end of the semester, the Dean at Talbot said they wanted to give me a farewell luncheon. I had attended several in the past and they were not pleasant. Usually it was for faculty who were not invited back, and I didn't want such a dismal experience. But the Dean insisted, and I am so glad he did. What a blessing it was. Over the course of 10 years I'd had the privilege to help a lot of my colleagues and their families. Most stopped by to wish me well. I thank God to this day that I got to leave on a high note.

That June we scheduled a three-day Freedom In Christ staff retreat at Arrowhead Springs. The first two days were just for our small staff and two couples whom we were considering. Those who were already on board were Dr. Tim and Eleanor Warner, Ron and Carole Wormser, and Jerry and Sally Friesen. Those we were considering were Robert and Grace Toews from Canada, and Carl and Esther Bobb from Switzerland. For two days we shared our lives with each other. Tim had been a missionary in Africa, the President of Fort Wayne Bible College, and the Director of the Doctor of Missions and Ministry program at Trinity Evangelical Divinity School. Both Tim and Eleanor had lost their first spouses to illness. Ron and Carole had just gone through a very difficult period of ministry, and their experience broadened my understanding of this fallen world. Jerry and Sally were just two beautiful Christian people. Carl Bobb was a United States citizen, a Talbot student of mine, who had previously worked for Torch Bearers in Austria. There he married Esther, a Swiss girl who worked with Torch Bearers as well.

We started with a core of broken people. Most of us had played the faculty games and suffered through ministry board wars, and didn't want any more of that. We were determined that this ministry was not going to have any prima donnas on staff, then or in the future. On the third day our newly formed board met with us, and they warmly accepted the Toews and the Bobbs to represent our ministry. The next day, Robert and Grace left for Canada to open the first foreign office for Freedom In Christ Ministries. The Bobbs did the same for Switzerland. Jerry and Sally would take care of our home office. Tim and Eleanor represented us around the world. Ron and Carole joined Joanne and myself as we traveled around the United States. We were off and running.

Isaac and Tara Manogarom were Biola University students from India. They met Jerry and Sally Friesen, who hosted foreign students in their home, and heard the message of Freedom In Christ. Isaac's father, Victor Manogarom, had recently retired from directing the Youth for Christ Ministry in India for many years. Isaac shared my first two books with his father and Victor said, "India has got to hear this message." So Victor came out of retirement and they all agreed to go back to India to set up an office for Freedom In Christ Ministries. Victor was well known in India and very well connected. He was the translator for Billy Graham at one of his crusades.

Then, out of the blue, I was asked to be the devotional speaker at a major evangelistic conference in Madras, India, where the Manogaroms planned to live. So the Manogaroms and I traveled to India the following January. Fifteen hundred evangelists attended this conference. I can't imagine a better way to launch a ministry. There was a prior event that made it even more meaningful.

Victory Over the Darkness and *The Bondage Breaker* were fresh off the press in June of 1990. Joanne and I were on our way to do a conference in Ames, Iowa. One of my students had just taken a position there, and heard that I was traveling in his direction. He called to ask if I would do a conference at their church. I said I could, so he asked the pastor, Dean Johnson, if that would be all right. Dean asked what the conference was about. When he heard that it had something to do with spiritual warfare, he flatly refused. With some persuasion he did agree to talk to me. I explained that it was about our identity in Christ, and how to resolve personal and spiritual conflicts through genuine repentance and faith in God. He agreed to have the conference.

Dean later became a district superintendent for the Evangelical Free Church, and became one of our best advocates. The leaders for another ministry in Ames, Iowa attended the conference, and they instigated the translation of *Victory Over the Darkness* and *The Bondage Breaker* into the Hindi language, which is the major language in India. So the Manogaroms had those two books available at the start of their ministry.

We drove through Denver on our way to Iowa and other

locations that summer. I heard that the Christian Booksellers Association (CBA) annual meeting was being held in Denver that year. So I called the editor at Harvest House to see if we could attend. They said that would be fine, and they would leave two tickets for Joanne and me at the reception desk. All the hotels in vicinity of the Denver convention center were booked up, so we had to drive in from the suburbs to attend CBA.

This was all new to me, so I had no idea what to expect. Most in attendance were representatives from Christian bookstores around the country. They were the customers. Every major Christian publisher was there, along with vendors who supplied bookstores with every kind of trinket imaginable. I was shocked. I thought CBA was for the selling of books. I learned that Christian bookstores can't stay in business just selling books, since that accounts for only about a quarter of their sales. Music, Bibles, and gifts make up the rest of their sales. The convention floor was totally covered by such vendors. Well-known Christian authors and artists were speaking and singing at plenary sessions and special functions organized by their publishers.

My first two books were newly in print, and I was tempted to think that I was a whale in a bathtub. I found out I was a minnow in a huge ocean. Joanne and I found the Gospel Light booth, but nobody recognized me, and I couldn't even find a copy of *Victory Over the Darkness*. There were stacks of books by well-known authors. Gospel Light had a new editor, who I hadn't met before. He came up to me and snapped his fingers twice trying to remember my name. Finally he said, "I think you are Neil Anderson, aren't you?" Then he snapped his finger two more times trying to remember what book I authored. Then someone important walked by and he had to leave. It was kind of humbling. That editor would later read the book, and it had a profound affect on him.

Next Joanne and I found the Harvest House booth, and the same editor who had contacted me originally greeted us saying, "Hi Neil, what are you doing here?" I reminded her that she had made the tickets available for us. They had only one copy of *The Bondage Breaker*, and that wasn't on display. I was disappointed to see the materialistic side of ministry. Every publisher is in competition to get books by certain well-known authors. Usually the authors have a radio or television ministry, or pastor huge churches. The first print run of their books would be in the tens of thousands. I had no recognizable name, no radio or TV ministry, and no large church, so nobody was expecting any big sales. However, to my surprise and that of my publishers, the books began to take off. Within months they were both bestsellers, and would continue to be for the next twenty plus years.

Six months later both publishers called to ask if I would come to CBA the following year at their expense. I said I would, but I also said that I was the same person I was last year. Both apologized for the previous year. I had to work this through in my mind. I was all about ministry; it seemed this industry was all about business. I began to understand that it had to be run as a business or they wouldn't be in business for long.

Harvest House Publishers asked me if I had another book in me, and I did. I had noticed for years that most of the adults that I was helping had had early childhood experiences that set them off in the wrong direction. Steve Russo, a youth evangelist, and I decided to do some research to determine what Christian teenagers were struggling with. So we surveyed 1,725 professing Christian teenagers (433 junior high school and 1,292 senior high school) attending Christian schools and camps. The first eight questions on the survey dealt with experiences that are common among people under demonic oppression. Question nine asked students about their participation in certain occult practices. The following figures indicate the percentage of students who answered "yes" to each question:

Question	Junior High	Senior High
1. Have you ever experienced (seen or heard) a presence in your room that scared you?	50%	47%
2. Do you struggle with bad thoughts about God?	44%	54%
3. Is it mentally hard for you to pray and read your Bible?	25%	37%
4. Have you heard a "voice" in your head like there was a subconscious self talking to you, or have struggled with really bad thoughts?	57%	70%
5. Have you frequently had thoughts of suicide?	12%	20%
6. Have you ever had impulsive thoughts to kill someone, like, "Grab that knife and kill that person?"	21%	24%
7. Have you ever thought you were different from others? (It works for others, but not for you)?	73%	71%
8. Do you like yourself?	89%	82%
9. Have you ever been involved with: Astral projection?	2%	2%
Table lifting?	8%	8%
Fortune telling?	8%	10%
Astrology?	11%	20%

"Dungeons and Dragons"?	18%	16%
Crystals or pyramids?	5%	3%
Ouija boards?	15%	26%
Automatic writing?	1%	2%
Tarot cards?	3%	6%
Palm reading?	7%	12%
Spirit guides?	1%	2%
Blood pacts?	3%	6%

This survey was reported in *The Seduction of Our Children* (Harvest House, 1991), which is now out of print. Those numbers have gotten far worse with the advent of the Internet and cell phones. According to recent reports, 20 per cent of the teenage population are "sexting," that is, taking pictures of their private parts and sending them by way of their phones. We considered writing a second edition of the book, and re-doing the research, but we couldn't get any churches or Christian schools to cooperate with us. In most cases their governing boards were split down the middle. Some saw this as an invasion of their privacy, while the others wanted to know what teenagers were struggling with so they could better support their children.

We have discovered that teenagers are far more interested in what we are teaching than their parents are. Five years after that research was reported, I was contacted by Peter and Sue Vander Hook. Peter was a pastor in an evangelical church, and they were seemingly doing everything right as parents. They marched for pro-life, home-schooled their children, and tried to live by faith according to the Bible. Suddenly they were having poltergeist type experiences in their home, and the children were having nightmares. They knew they were in a spiritual battle, but didn't know where to go for help.

They came across my first two books, and were able to finally help their children. In the process they both discovered who they were in Christ, and learned how to help others in their church. They tell their story in a book, which they co-authored with me entitled, *Spiritual Protection For Your Children* (Regal Books, 1995). The book includes age-graded Steps to Freedom for children, which can be downloaded from our ministry's website (www.ficm.org).

Several years later, the ministry of Youth for Christ in England asked if we would do a youth version of our discipleship course with them, which we did. It was filmed in thirteen different locations in England. A male and a female staff member from Youth for Christ presented the message, which is being used widely in the United States and the United Kingdom. If the future of our countries rests on the shoulders of the next generation, how important is it that they are established alive and free in Christ?

15

Corporate Conflict Resolution

One day in Portiuncula, while at prayer alone in his cell, St. Francis saw a vision of the whole house surrounded and besieged by devils. They were like a great army surrounding the place, but none of them could gain entrance to the house. The brothers were so disciplined and devoted in their lives of sanctity that the devils were frustrated without a host upon whom they might find a way in.

It happened, in the days soon after Francis's vision, that one of the brothers became offended by another and he began to think in his heart of ways to revenge the slight. While the scheming brother was devising vengeful plans, entertaining wicked thoughts, the devil, finding an open door, entered Portiuncula upon his back.

Francis, the watchful shepherd of his flock, saw that the wolf had entered, intending to devour his little sheep. At once, Francis called the brother to him and asked him to disclose the hatred that had caused this disturbance in his house. The brother, frightened that Francis knew the content of

> *his heart, disclosed to him all of the venom and malice that consumed him, acknowledging his fault and begging humbly for forgiveness.*
>
> *Loving his sheep as does his Father, the shepherd soon absolved the brother, and immediately, at that moment, before his very face, Francis saw the devil flee from his presence. The brother returned to the flock and the wolf was gone from the house.*[11]

I have had similar experiences, but one in particular stands out in my mind. We were kicking off a conference one Sunday morning in Louisiana. Between the Sunday morning services I asked the pastor, "Do you want to talk about it?" "Talk about what?" he asked. I said, "What's going on here?" "Is it that obvious?" he asked. I told him, "My Bible fell off the pulpit in the first service, and it hasn't hit the ground yet! The air is so thick you can cut it with a knife." Joanne and Carole Wormser were up the in balcony praying. The spiritual atmosphere changed for the good on Monday evening. It was so noticeable that people commented on it throughout the conference. The source of the problem became evident. Two of the associate staff were in the bondage of bitterness. One thought he should have been the senior pastor, and proceeded to poison the spirit of the other staff member, which clouded the spiritual atmosphere of the whole church.

For years I had been helping individuals who were living in bondage to lies and bitterness. Freedom came when they genuinely repented and believed the truth. The answer was not to get rid of the flies, but to get rid of the garbage. So I started to wonder if

---

11 Paul Sabatier, *The Road to Assisi: The Essential Biography of St. Francis* (Brewster, MA: Paraclete Press, 2003). page 167.

there is such a thing as corporate garbage, and therefore a need for corporate repentance?

When I did that first videotaping mentioned in chapter 13, a pastor, John Tabay, attended the whole week with his staff. At the end of the week, he asked me if I thought there was such a thing as corporate bondage. Over twnety-five years earlier, a church had gone through an ugly split. A year later John accepted an invitation to be the pastor of the splinter group, but it hadn't been easy. He told me that the original people who were part of the split were long since gone, but the challenge to his leadership continued – the garbage was still there. If this was a corporate problem, how should he deal with it? We discussed various possibilities of bringing the issue to the light and corporately repenting. So he preached on the matter, and called the congregation to repent of their past sins on a Sunday evening. A year later I asked him how it went. He said, "This past year has been our best year by far. I haven't had the usual opposition to my leadership."

Dr. Charles (Chuck) Mylander was the district superintendent of the Friends churches in Southern California. He had recently experienced some fruit using the Steps to Freedom on a missionary trip, and I had helped someone close to him on a personal level. We were discussing this over lunch when the subject of corporate conflict resolution came up. He oversaw several churches that were prime candidates for such help if we only knew how to do it. Unless some of these churches came to terms with their past, they probably had no future.

Many of the apostle Paul's letters are written to churches. Christians have a personal relationship with God, but do they also have a corporate relationship with God? I could help individuals be established alive and free in Christ, but where would they go to church afterwards? The question is similar to that we face with children. We could help a teenager resolve their personal and spiritual conflicts, and then what? Send them back to a dysfunctional family, which contributed to their problem in the first place? One obviously affects the other. If a church is full of people who are living in bondage to sin, the whole church is in bondage. If a church has mostly bad marriages, you have a bad church. The whole cannot be greater than the summation of its parts. So where do you start?

It has to start with the leadership. People cannot rise above their leaders, and God created the church to be led by godly elders and deacons. The author of Hebrews wrote, "Obey your leaders and submit to them, for they are keeping watch over your souls, as those who will have to give an account. Let them do this with joy and not with groaning, for that would be of no advantage to you" (13:17 ESV). With that in mind, Chuck and I turned to the book of Revelation and developed a means of corporate conflict resolution based on the seven letters to the seven churches. Every letter ends with the same statement, "He who has an ear, let him hear what the Spirit says to the churches" (Revelation 2:7 and following verses, ESV). God is calling His churches to repent, but are we listening? Notice the spiritual overtones in several of the churches:

> *To Smyrna: I know your tribulation and your poverty (but you are rich) and the slander of those who say that they are Jews and are not, but are a synagogue of Satan.*
>
> Revelation 2:9 ESV

What people saw were Jews who slandered the Christians in the Smyrna church. What Jesus saw was a "synagogue of Satan." What people saw were Roman rulers who threw Christians in jail. What Jesus saw was the devil who put some of them in prison. These enemies of the gospel were doing the devil's work by attacking the church in Smyrna. What people see and what Jesus sees are quite different. Since every action is preceded by a thought, where are those thoughts coming from?

> *To Pergamum: I know where you dwell, where Satan's throne is. Yet you hold fast my name, and you did not deny my faith even in the days of Antipas my faithful witness, who was killed among you, where Satan dwells.*
>
> Revelation 2:13 ESV

What people saw was a city on a hill with major temples in it. What Jesus saw was Satan's throne. What people saw was the center of emperor worship in the Ancient Near East. What Jesus saw was the city where Satan lived. This place was oppressive to Christians.

> *To Thyatira: But to the rest of you in Thyatira, who do not hold this teaching, who have not learned what some call the deep things of Satan, to you I say, I do not lay on you any other burden. Only hold fast what you have until I come.*
>
> Revelation 2:24–25 ESV

What people saw was a prophetess who taught that since grace covered every sin, it was OK to indulge in pagan temple feasts. What Jesus saw was Satan's deceptive secrets for indulging sexual sin and satanic rituals. The church at Philadelphia also had to contend with a "synagogue of Satan" (Revelation 3:9). With no means of resolving corporate sins churches will likely end up being lukewarm like the church in Laodicea. "So because you are lukewarm, and neither hot nor cold, I will spit you out of my mouth" (Revelation 3:16 ESV). In other words, we can't expect God's favor if we are not living righteous lives, corporately or individually.

My role in the process was to explain servant leadership and corporate structure. If we managed to resolve the conflicts and didn't address those issues the church would likely fall back into its old patterns. If the pastor was a legalistic dictator and remained one, nothing really got resolved. If the church had four boards and poor communication, unless that changed the same problems would likely surface again. Chuck, being a district superintendent, had churches we could work with. Just as Christ is the Wonderful Counselor in individual counselling, we believe that He is the ultimate Church Consultant. We are dealing with His body, and the key is to get the church leaders to listen to what the Holy Spirit is saying and repent. God Himself would write the letter to their church. In the seven letters written to the seven churches of Revelation, the singular, "I" occurs over fifty times, and "I" is Christ. He is present in all our churches and He knows them in a way that we could never know.

After Chuck had tried our approach on seventeen of his churches, we invited the pastors to come together and share their stories and offer suggestions. With their feedback we wrote the book, *Setting Your Church Free* (Regal Books, 1994). Later we wrote a second edition, entitled, *Extreme Church Makeover* (Regal Books, 2005). I had the privilege to lead many churches through the process, as have Freedom In Christ staff around the world, with exciting results. I also led a denomination, a seminary, and two parachurch ministries through the process. I taught a Doctor of Ministry class at Trinity Evangelical Divinity School on the subject of Setting Your Church Free, and they had to turn students away. Almost every pastor that attended had a horror story to tell. Over time we noticed that the churches asking for help were good churches that wanted to get better. Sick churches didn't call us, because the leadership would not submit to the process, as the following testimony illustrates:

> *In 1993 I purchased a set of your tapes. After listening to these tapes I began applying your principles to my problems. I realized that some of my problems could be spiritual attacks, and I learned how to take a stand and won some victories over problems in my life.*
>
> *This is only a tip of the iceberg. I'm a deacon and preacher in a Baptist church. My pastor was suffering from depression and other problems that I was not aware of and in 1994 he committed suicide. This literally brought our church to its knees. I knew some of the problems of the previous pastors and felt it was spiritual, but I didn't know how to relay it to the people, since the Devil or a demon cannot affect a Christian; "RIGHT."*
>
> *The church elected me as their interim pastor. While in a local bookstore I saw a book of yours on Setting Your Church Free. I purchased and read it. I felt with all the spiritual suppression in our church this was the answer. Only one problem: to get the rest of the church to believe. After a few weeks of preaching on spiritual things, I knew we had to act on your Setting Your Church Free. The previous pastor that killed himself would not believe your material, he would never read or listen to your message.*

Slowly, very slowly the people accepted my messages and I was able to contact one of your staff. He flew to Houston and led the leaders of our church through "the Steps to Setting Your Church Free." The leaders loved it. I felt step one was past. Next I wanted to take all the people through "The Steps to Freedom In Christ." Six weeks later, I was able to do so. I really don't understand it, but we were set free from the spiritual bondage of multiple problems. Can't put it in a letter, or I would write a book.

During all this one of my middle-aged members, who is an evangelist, was set free; learned who he is in Christ and is back in ministry. Praise the Lord! I saw the twin daughters of the deceased pastor set free and forgive their father. The twin girls were able to get on with their lives. At one point, one of the twins was contemplating suicide.

This is a new church; God is free to work here! In September we founded our pulpit committee. Our church voted 100 percent for our new pastor. This has never happened in our church before, and this is an independent, fundamental, Baptist Church. Well, when you do things God's way, you get God's results.

I have all of your material, and I love your ministry. I work one night a week in our county jail with the homosexual men, and I have seen some of the men set free.

Over the years we have learned that individual leaders must be established alive and free in Christ before they can effectively work through corporate issues. So Chuck and I wondered if this same process could be used for marriages? Were we trying to resolve marital problems when only one, or neither spouse is free? Can a couple be one in Christ, if one or neither is right with God?

While conducting Living Free In Christ conferences, people would talk to me about their marriages. After hearing their story I would say, "Forget your marriage. You are so torn up on the inside that you probably couldn't get along with your dog right now. Finish this conference for one reason and one reason only, which is to resolve your own personal and spiritual conflicts." As a result many have walked out hand in hand with their spouse, and we have hardly mentioned the subject of marriage.

The apostle Paul's epistles have a common order. The first half deals with theological issues and the second half is practical, that is the indicative precedes the imperative (being before doing). Christian counselors are practical people and they want to help their clients live out their roles as parents, husbands, and wives. Consequently most of their instruction comes from the Old Testament and the second half of Paul's epistles. Many churches and ministries are offering marriage seminars, parenting seminars, single parenting seminars, and so on. There are so many books on the subject that one doesn't know how to choose. The most-listened to Christian radio ministry is Focus on the Family. Never in the history of the world has there been a more concerted effort to help the family. How we doing?

Most of this material is biblical and needed so what is the problem? Did we get the cart before the horse? It seems like we have many good and necessary spokes in the Christian wheel, but they may not be connected to the hub. What did the first half of Paul's epistles do? They established you in Christ. If we can help believers enter into the first half of Paul's epistles, they will do the second half supernaturally. We have tried to help them act like Christians when they are not firmly rooted in Christ, but Christianity is not an act. It is a real relationship with the Creator, and if we are fully reconciled to Him, then we can be reconciled to each other. "We love because He first loved us" (1 John 4:19). What we have freely received, we freely give to one another. "Be kind to one another, tenderhearted, forgiving one another, as God in Christ forgave you" (Ephesians 4:32 ESV). We can't bear fruit unless we abide in Christ. When we are first connected to the hub of the wheel, then all the spokes are energized and we can do the work of God. Trying to do that in our own strength and resources doesn't work.

The problem is, we didn't marry Adam or Eve before the fall. We married one of their fallen descendants. And men, we didn't just marry that sweet little thing, we got her weird brother, her sick uncle, a mother-in-law and three plus generations of habits, customs, and traditions. Should either spouse have any unresolved issues in their past, they bring those with them as well. Some do so hoping that marriage will resolve things for them, but just the opposite happens. Marriage exposes their character defects, and they bounce off each other's wounds, unless they are healed in Christ. We need to bring the ultimate Marriage Counselor into the process and see what happens.

Essentially Chuck and I followed the same process for marriages as we did for churches. God is always present, so let's start the process by having each spouse pray and ask for God's guidance. Then comes the hard part. Neither spouse can deal with the other person's issues. They cannot play the role of the Holy Spirit in each other's life. Nobody is keeping the husband or wife from being the person God created them to be, except themselves. We have to be responsible for ourselves and for what we brought into the marriage. The process breaks down when only one is trying. So we developed the Steps to Setting Your Marriage

Free with three different editions. The first one is Beginning Your Marriage Free, which the engaged person can work through on their own. Wouldn't it be great if everyone began their marriage with no baggage from their past? The second one is for the spouse who has a partner who won't cooperate entitled, When Only One Will Try. The third is for both husband and wife.

I was doing a Doctor of Ministry Class at Talbot School of Theology on Discipleship Counseling. One pastor enrolled in the class as a skeptic, and didn't hide it very well from the rest of the students. They were given an option. They could write a paper or attend our first ever Setting Your Marriage Free event a month later. They all chose the latter.

We held the conference at a major hotel, and around 300 attended. To do the conference well, it would take Friday evening and all day Saturday. I gave some instruction, explained each step and how to do it, had them all pray with me in a corporate setting, and then each spouse would sit silently and listen. After they had dealt with their own personal issues, they would go to their rooms as a couple and share with each other. Sometimes that meant confessing their sins to one another, and asking their spouse to forgive them. Unfortunately the hotel only had two elevators, which created a traffic jam.

After the fifth step one couple didn't leave the plenary session. He had his arm draped over her shoulder and both were looking downcast. So I said to them, "I can see that it is not working for you. Obviously you know why. Would you care to share that with me?" She said, "You told us that we couldn't deal with our spouse's issues, but what do we do if they won't deal with them?" So I asked him, "Is there an issue more important to you than your marriage?" He said, "I suppose she would say it is my drinking, and I have tried to deal with that, but it didn't work." I explained why the secular program he had tried couldn't set him free, and he received that, but there was nothing more that could be done that day. That really underscored how important it is to work through individual problems first. They probably could have resolved their marital issues if he had given her some hope that he would at least try a grace-based ministry of overcoming addictive behavior.

My seminary skeptic chose to come to the marriage conference rather than write a paper, but he still had to give me a final report. He had become a believer in the message. Prior to the conference he and his wife used to get into a major argument every Sunday morning before they went to church. It had been going on for years. It got so bad that they dreaded Sundays. Neither had a clue that there could be a spiritual base for this problem. Many other issues were resolved during that conference, and Sunday mornings were peaceful from that time on.

The next time I tried the Setting Your Marriage Free conference, it was in a church. The hotel worked well for giving individual couples a confidential place to work together in their private rooms. The church building was less conducive for this, especially on our first attempt. We had 240 couples come. So they had to spread out around the auditorium and use every corner in every classroom in the church. When I dismissed them to do so on the first night, a lady approached me with her husband trailing far behind. She said he would not cooperate, so I asked him why. He said, "I am not going to laugh at your jokes, or do what you say!" I said, "That is fine with me, but you are not ready for this conference." I offered to give their registration fee back. When they left I was pretty sure I that I would never see them again. To my surprise they actually did stay throughout the whole conference and approached me at the end on Saturday afternoon with smiles on their faces. God keeps showing me that He is bigger than my expectations.

I was doing the marriage conference in a Lutheran church in Canada. We asked all those who signed up to come on Friday afternoon to go through the individual Steps to Freedom if they had never done so before. An attractive young lady came by herself, and went through the Steps to Freedom. The Setting Your Marriage Free seminar began that night at 7:00 p.m., and she was still by herself. So I met with her when the couples were meeting with each other. I found out that she had been raised a Catholic and her husband had been raised a Baptist. Her husband suggested they compromise and become members of a Christian and Missionary Alliance church. That wasn't much of a compromise for him!

Her husband had finished medical school and was interning at a hospital and couldn't get that weekend off. They were struggling in their marriage, and she took most of the blame upon herself. In this case I think she was right. He sounded like a very committed Christian, and she less so. In our first meeting I listened to her story. In our second meeting I led her to Christ. In the subsequent meetings I took her through the individual steps, and the marriage steps that applied. At the end of the conference she was a different person, and just glowed with the love of Christ. I wonder what her husband thought when she came home that evening.

At that same conference, a wife suddenly left, leaving her husband there by himself. We had come to the step that deals with sexual sins. I dismiss the wives with some assignments for them to do on their own, and then talk to the men. After a half hour, the men are dismissed and I talk to the wives. The purpose is to give them an opportunity to resolve any sexual issues between themselves and God. Then the couple meet together to resolve any issues that still exist between them. That was when his wife left the conference.

When the husband told me that she had left, I asked him why. He said, "Two years ago my wife had an affair, and we have been trying to work through this. After going through this process today, I felt convicted that I needed to tell her that I have been having an affair for ten years." I didn't have to slug him, God already had. I said, "If I were you I would go running after her, and beg her forgiveness."

After conducting a few conferences on Setting Your Marriage Free, I decided that this ministry belongs in the local church. We encourage churches to offer our basic discipleship course first, and then offer a class on marriage using our book, *Experiencing Christ Together* (Regal Books, 2006). They can schedule their own conference on a Friday evening and finish on Saturday. That way the groups are smaller, and better prepared.

There is no way that I would ever ask anyone to do something that I wouldn't do myself. So Joanne and I took a day to work through the process ourselves, as did Chuck and his wife, Nancy. We are both happily married to our first spouses, but each of us hit some rough spots during the process. I suspect that every couple would discover some discrepancies, since nobody is perfect. But that shouldn't stop us from letting God examine our hearts, and be willing to let Him show us our shortfalls.

As a ministry, we have gone through the Setting Your Church Free process three times. The first time Freedom In Christ was a young ministry. There were no outstanding moral issues to be resolved, and the ministry was small enough for every staff person and their spouse to be included in the process. It was the wives who spoke up and made us aware of our biggest weakness: we had become driven, and hadn't learned how to say no. The United States office would go through the process again after I stepped down as the U.S. President of the ministry. They would need to do it again, when the next President resigned. On a personal level, we clean our own house every time we take another person through the Steps. Every time we help another person, we help ourselves. It is one of life's greatest compensations. The more we give, the more we receive.

16

Growing Pains

In the early nineties Campus Crusade for Christ invited me to present the Freedom In Christ conference in Singapore. Victor Koh was the Asian Director at that time, and he encouraged their top leaders and staff to attend the conference. When it was over, Victor and some of his key leaders took us out for dinner. Their question was, "How do we get the church in America to see what you are teaching?" I have been asked similar questions in my travels overseas. Some are even surprised that an American evangelical is even acknowledging the reality of the spiritual world. The Christian exportation of western rationalism and naturalism is not very well received in many parts of the world.

On the way home from that trip, we were discussing the possibility of recording a freedom appointment. The process surfaces a lot of intimate issues that most would not like others to see. So who would be willing to do that? A lady's name did come to our minds. She had been hospitalized three times for depression. When she had previously heard me speak about the battle for our minds, she had requested help. So we asked her if she would be willing to help out, and she agreed. In two hours she went from a clinically depressed person, to a liberated child of God. Her countenance was completely different at the end. That DVD was the best training tool that we had for years.

Meanwhile, our staff team was growing, and it put a lot of strain on the US office. Jerry had sold his business to get out of management, and now he was up to his armpits in alligators again. The husband of the lady mentioned above had lost his job, so we offered him an administrative staff position to help Jerry. It was a sympathy decision that didn't work out. Not knowing how to hire the right people to help us, almost undid us. Frankly, I was just too trusting, and I would let almost anybody be a part of what we were doing. Thankfully that has changed over the years, and steps have been made to ensure that the right people are doing the right ministry.

Invitations were coming in rapid succession in those early years. We were seeing so much fruit that I thought we should be prepared for some opposition. At a staff retreat I gave some talks on the supernatural ministries of Elijah and Elisha, and the opposition they faced. The possibility of my doing a radio ministry was being proposed by some of the staff. I didn't know anything about radio, and I wasn't going to consider that option unless someone came along with the right skills and a million dollars. I was not going to raise any money to keep this ministry going. My view has always been, if God wants it to continue He will supply the resources. If He doesn't, the ministry is over.

The next week a man from Florida called our office. His wife was a Christian psychologist and she thought our message was the best she had ever seen for helping people. They wanted to fly to California with their adopted son who needed some help. The plan was for one of our staff to meet with the son, with his mother sitting in on the session. This man didn't have a radio station; he owned a television network. He didn't have a million dollars; he had many millions of dollars. He wanted to put me and the message on television at his expense. God doesn't take His time testing His children!

Several of us met with him in our workroom. Joanne was the most discerning person present, and she was so turned off that she couldn't even look at him after a matter of minutes. He picked up on it and asked if he had offended her. All but one of us knew the matter was closed within minutes, and so we chatted awkwardly for almost three hours. I was thankful that God had prepared us the week before, because the opportunity was tempting. For the discerning it sounded too much like the devil showing Jesus all the kingdoms of the world and saying, "All this will I give you" (Matthew 4:8–9).

That wasn't the biggest test, however. A nationally syndicated radio ministry was publicly criticizing me. The host was telling people to burn *The Bondage Breaker*. They published a journal and printed four inflammatory articles about me. In the first article, entitled "The Bondage Maker," I was "a New Age, Catholic, Robert Schuller." The slander continued for several years. When the negative criticism first started, I was surprised and thought it was just a misunderstanding. I had twice been a guest on this radio program, and I knew several of the staff. Some were former students of mine. So I sent them a number of my books and tapes hoping that would clarify the issue, but the negative criticism only increased.

No attempt was ever made to contact me before or during this period of criticism. So I made an appointment to see the host along with Dr. Robert Saucy. He was on the board of Freedom In Christ Ministries at that time, and held the position of Distinguished Professor of Systematic Theology at Talbot School of Theology. Unfortunately Dr. Saucy had to cancel so we rescheduled another meeting a month later. To my surprise and disappointment, the public criticism increased before we could even meet. So I canceled the second meeting, and decided that I had little recourse but to forgive the host and move on.

The radio station also published a position paper on our ministry, which gave a very false impression of who we are and what we believe. Since we all have blind spots and can occasionally make mistakes we are not aware of, I sent the paper to twenty-five churches and ministries that had sponsored Freedom In Christ Ministry events, and asked for their feedback. In the letter, which I copied to the radio ministry, I said:

> *As you may know, I wish not to be defensive in what I believe God has called me to say. Therefore, my first response is to ask myself if there is any truth in their critique of the message of Freedom In Christ. If any portion of what they say were true, then I would definitely need to repent. On the other hand, if what they're saying is not true, then such a critique would be damaging to both our ministries. I believe in my own heart that what we present in our conferences is almost the opposite of what they report... I would appreciate a candid response from you on their statement. If you feel led to do so, please send your response to their ministry as well... Please feel free to be honest with me about any concerns you may have of our ministry. We're committed to the truth and to the unity of the body of Christ.*

I received no corrective feedback. It would grieve me if I learned that I had wrongly criticized another person's ministry, but in this case it only served to double their efforts. The editor of their journal had searched for someone to do the articles about our ministry. One person they contacted had formerly been on staff with them. He was also a former student of mine at Talbot School of Theology who happened to agree with me, and he called to inform me what they were going to do. Apparently, the editor couldn't find someone else, so he decided to do the first three articles in the journal, and these were followed up with radio programs.

Now other Christian leaders were being questioned for endorsing my books, so for their sake I needed to do something. I appealed to the National Religious Broadcasters (NRB). I informed them what was going on, and asked them to choose three credible theologians to examine both my message and me. If I were found to be wrong, I would publicly apologize. The matter was referred to the ethics committee and their chairman asked if I would meet with the host of the radio program accompanied by a member of the committee.

A registered letter was sent to them requesting a meeting. When there was no response, a second registered letter was sent. I flew to California for the two days we had set aside, but their host had no intention of meeting with us. We informed NRB that we had fulfilled our responsibility and were not going to pursue the matter any further. They expressed their disappointment that the host would not meet with us, and thanked me for following through with the recommendation even though it produced no results.

The matter was not settled for me, however. I still wanted to meet with some respected and neutral theologians for the sake of my own ministry. Dr. Robert Saucy contacted three well-known theologians. They were each given copies of the journal articles and transcripts of the broadcasts. They also read five of my books: *Victory Over The Darkness, The Bondage Breaker, Helping Others Find Freedom In Christ, Finding Hope Again,* and *The Common Made Holy.*

We met on a Friday afternoon and Saturday morning, for the purpose of discussing my theology. The radio host was sent a registered letter inviting him to come. The response we received explained his absence:

> *We are accountable before men, and we would be very willing to have our criticism of your theology judged by the larger body of Christ, say, in a public, advertised debate (to which the leading evangelical magazines and scholarly journals would be invited) between you and Dr. Saucy on the one hand and ourselves on the other. But our conscience is bound in the word of God, and we therefore will never submit to having truth determined by the vote of a panel of three theologians selected by the NRB who may or may not be as competent as we are to judge these matters.*

This is pretty tough talk when the host hadn't even completed a college degree, much less a seminary degree. To this day, they have not called, or written to me or my office, for the purpose of setting up a meeting to discuss my message or ministry. In order to conduct quality research, one must remove all personal bias and go directly to the source. That certainly was not done. Christian ethics require the believer to talk first with the wayward individual before going public. This simple procedure gives the wayward brother a chance to repent and hopefully clarify any misunderstandings. If that doesn't work, then make another visit with two other witnesses. If that doesn't work, then tell the church. To tell the church without going to the person first shows no regard for the other person or their reputation.

It would be grounds for dismissal if one of my staff publicly criticized other ministries without going to them first. If the host had concerns about my message, why didn't he come talk to me instead of throwing out public challenges on the radio program and in their journal? Paul wrote, "Let no unwholesome word proceed from your mouth, but only such a word as is good for edification according to the need of the moment, so that it will give grace to those who hear. Do not grieve the Holy Spirit of God, by whom you were sealed for the day of redemption" (Ephesians 4:29–30 NASB). It grieves God when He sees His children putting one another down when we should be building one another up.

Grief is my response as well. It grieves me to see brothers and sisters in Christ attacking one another. Paul continues; "Let all bitterness and wrath and anger and clamor and slander be put away from you, along with all malice. Be kind to one another, tender-hearted, forgiving each other, just as God in Christ has forgiven you" (Ephesians 4:31–32 NASB). I have chosen to forgive this man, and so has our staff. Jesus said we are to bless those who curse us, and that is what we will do by the grace of God. I believe I have no other biblical obligation with regard to their radio program.

I attended the meeting with the three theologians with plans already underway to write second editions of *Victory Over The Darkness* and *The Bondage Breaker.* So their feedback was valuable to me in finishing the second editions, published in the year 2000. We all wished we could have met under less painful conditions, and I am grateful for their gracious concern for the body of Christ and the contribution they made. In their final report they wrote:

> *In our judgment, Anderson stands well within the bounds of Christian orthodoxy, and in no respect do we consider his teachings heretical... We believe that the treatment of sanctification and growth in holiness presented in Dr. Anderson's and Dr. Saucy's recent book,* The Common Made Holy *(1997), represents a more biblically nuanced and balanced treatment on the subject versus earlier works, such as* Victory Over The Darkness *(1990), and* The Bondage Breaker *(1990). Critics should recognize the development in Dr. Anderson's thinking, which by his own admission, is currently taking place.*

I am too anecdotal, was another criticism that I have heard. In truth I do have a lot of experience helping others find their freedom in Christ through genuine repentance, and I have certainly learned from my experiences. My experience of growing in Christ and ministering with others has caused me to grow in my understanding of the Bible, but shouldn't it? I look to the Bible for answers and I have always believed that God's word is the sole authority for faith and practice. It seems like those who use the anecdotal argument have no anecdotal experiences to share themselves.

Theology is man's attempt to systematize truth. Over the last thirty years of ministry, my theology has changed. The truth hasn't changed, but my understanding of the truth has changed and it will continue to change if I am growing. There is an old saying that a man with an argument has no chance against a man with experience. One may think they have a good theological argument, but until they have sat with hurting people and learned how the truth sets them free, all they have is an argument. James says, "But prove yourselves doers of the word, and not merely hearers who delude themselves" (James 1:22 NASB). I haven't really grown until I actually live according to the word of God. My theology has been affected by my experience of growing and ministering to others and being ministered to. Hasn't yours?

According to Jesus the proof is in the fruit you bear. Some may think they know all things, but if they have no love they are only a "noisy gong or a clanging cymbal" (1 Corinthians 13:1 ESV). Paul says the goal of our instruction is love (1 Timothy 1:5). Jesus said, "By this all men will know that you are My disciples, if you have love for one another" (John 13:35 NASB). Jesus said, "So then, you will know them by their fruits" (Matthew 7:20 NASB).

There probably is another reason some may think I form my theology from my experience. I share a lot of testimonies and read letters that people have sent me. Some may think I am taking a few exceptional cases and extrapolating the results to the general population. I share those letters and testimonies for the purpose of illustrating the truth I am teaching. To some that is being anecdotal. I disagree. Jesus was a storyteller and illustrator, and stories and good illustrations enhance the learning experience. Christians should never have to apologize for a good testimony. I received the following unsolicited testimony from someone who attended one of my conferences, and apparently was aware of the slander:

> *I was at a Freedom In Christ seminar last weekend and you are right, Neil Anderson is not perfect. He is just like you and I. But he said some things that I really needed to hear. It was things that I knew intellectually, but it's as if someone did not*

want me to understand it for years. The man talked at a small church (I don't think there were more than 200 people present) and he was there with all his heart, Wednesday night through Friday night and all day Saturday. He also had a seminar on Discipleship Counseling during the day on Thursday and Friday. The cost was only 25 dollars. His philosophy is, "Why should I get paid for what God does in people's lives." I met him personally and he took time to talk with me and answer my questions even though he was really busy that evening. Very nice guy!!

As far as the disagreement the radio ministry has with Neil Anderson, I don't see a case there. But even if Anderson is mistaken somewhere, I don't know anyone even close who is out there tackling the issues that he is – and actually setting people free. It would be a shame if some struggling Christian or an unbeliever were kept away as a result of one of their articles. Why not just address the same issues and let the people decide on who's teaching correctly and who isn't? By the way, it's not right for a Christian to use sarcasm like this: "The Bondage Maker?" That is not only untrue, it tells me something is not right in his heart.

I noticed that Neil Anderson does not use his platform to critique others – much less where in the Bible a case can be made either way. But he is going around the country setting people free in Christian love. I thank the Lord for this man; he is a blessing. I just bought another book of his, and I REALLY recommend his seminars to everyone. "Holding on to bitterness is like swallowing poison and hoping the other person will die." I learned that at the conference too.

I am still puzzled to this day why this attack from the radio program even happened. What possible harm was I doing? What is the worst thing that can happen if you take a person through the Steps to Freedom In Christ? You can't hurt a person with the process, their wounds could be healed, and they just might be set free from their past. Plus, they are really going to be ready to participate in communion the next Sunday.

For those who are concerned about my theology, I encourage them to visit our website (www.ficm.org). I have answered the most common questions that we receive. Also, I have written a practical systematic theology entitled, *The Daily Discipler* (Regal Books, 2005).

Trying to keep my heart free from bitterness was a struggle, however. Several times I have thought about quitting. I thought, *I don't need this.* One fall I had over-extended myself. I was on the road from mid-September to the middle of November with only brief stops at home. I was tired of the travel and here I was doing another conference in Canada. It started with two sessions on a Wednesday evening. Between the sessions I went out in the hallway just to be alone for a couple of minutes. A scruffy-looking character came up to me and said, "God says I am supposed to pray for you." I asked, "Do I need prayer?" He said, "You do. You have fiery darts all over you." Usually I'm a little skeptical of such offerings, but this time I sensed he was right. He proceeded to pray very authoritatively about those fiery darts. When he was done I actually felt refreshed. I asked Clay Bergen, our Canadian director, "Who was that guy?" Clay said, "He is John the Baptist," without a hint of derision. This man was quite well known in Regina as a man of prayer. He didn't have a job and wasn't looking for one. He just prayed, and the churches supported him. What a blessing.

The radio slander and libel did have an impact on our ministry. Conferences were canceled, and we had to scale down our ministry in the States. But there is a silver lining in every cloud. God used this to expand our ministry overseas. As a result the message is far better known in Europe, Africa, Asia, and South America. I still did training in the United States when invited, but the real expansion was happening overseas. The best church example is in Columbia, South America.

Dario Silva-Silva was a journalist with connections in the circles of power in Bogota, Colombia, in South America. Needing financial assistance he was connected with Esther Lucia who was instrumental in leading Dario to the feet of Christ. They later married and started the Casa Sobre La Roca church. Dario also played a leading role in changing the constitution of Colombia granting religious freedom.

Apparently the message of Freedom In Christ played a role in the establishment of their church. Dario informed me that he had prayed for two years that I would come to Colombia and speak at their home church on their tenth anniversary, which I did. I was informed that all those who made a decision for Christ were taught the message of Freedom In Christ and led through the Steps to Freedom In Christ. On their tenth anniversary their home church had 3,000 members and they had started seven other churches. Over the next two years, I returned and did some further training at the home church as well as their churches in Cali and Armenia, Colombia.

I was again invited to speak at their twentieth anniversary. By then the home church had grown to nearly 10,000, and they now have thirty-four churches. In July of 2011 I did my final conference at the home church. Two thousand attended and it was shown simultaneously to all the other churches.

The Casa Sobre la Roca churches are the healthiest churches that I have had the privilege to work with anywhere in the world. They are well disciplined, and every attendee is fully engaged during the service. No other churches or denominations model better what I teach. Every Sunday scores of people come forward to receive Christ. They are taught who they are in Christ and led through a repentance process (the Steps). Then they are baptized and admitted into the church. That is what the early church did.

I take no credit for that. Dario is an educated and intelligent leader who loves his people. After hearing my final seminar, he claimed that what I taught was his position too. He said, "I am a Baptist on steroids and a Pentecostal with the brakes on." The heart of the church is missionary and they care for their people. About 15 per cent of their Sunday morning offering goes to support ten homes for orphans and displaced children that were founded by Esther Lucia. After the conference I visited for the second time the principle center of the orphanages managed by the main church in Bogota. They had a big sign welcoming me, and I sat there with tears in my eyes as a teenage representative shared how the message of Freedom In Christ changed her life and she now knows who she is in Christ.

Since these children come from the streets and abandoned homes, I asked what kind of mental and emotional problems they continue to struggle with. The director said, "Almost none at all. Every child above the age of four is taken through the Steps to Freedom and taught who they are in Christ and how to live by faith in the power of the Holy Spirit." The lead counselor and teacher also thanked me for the material, which she uses with all the children. These orphanages are the cleanest and best administered homes that I have ever seen. Two former orphans gave me a guided tour. One had just graduated from college and the other was in her second year of engineering. It is the most beautiful expression of Christian love that I have witnessed anywhere.

It can happen in your church. Jesus said, "Repent and believe in the gospel" (Mark 1:15 ESV), and the apostle Paul preached repentance everywhere he went. People come to Christ by faith, but they need to repent if they are going to become reproducing disciples. Once they are established alive and free in Christ, then they can grow in the grace of God and bear much fruit.

17

Recovery in Christ

When I was teaching at Talbot School of Theology, I offered an elective on advanced pastoral counseling. We would study various approaches to difficult issues such as chemical and sexual addiction. One of their assignments was to attend an Alcoholics Anonymous (AA) meeting, and give a written report. The seminary students didn't care much for the smoking and the coarse language, but most said, "I wish the people who attended our Bible studies at church were that honest about their problems."

For several years I invited Bob and Pauline Bartosh to share their testimony in the class. They were the founders of Overcomers Outreach, which was a ministry for those struggling with chemical addictions. Essentially they offered the AA Twelve-Step Program in a Christian setting. I was interested to know what Bob Bartosh made of *Freedom From Addiction* (Regal Books, 1996), a book I co-authored with Mike and Julia Quarles when they joined our ministry. The first half of the book is Mike and Julia's story of their recovery in Christ, and in the second half of the book I present a theology for overcoming addictive behavior, which is now available as a book by itself: *Overcoming Addictive Behavior* (Regal Books, 2003). I shared the first half of the book with Bob Bartosh, and asked for his feedback. He wasn't too happy with it!

Bob believed that alcoholics were born that way and would always be alcoholics, and said, "In all my years of helping alcoholics I have never seen any evidence of the demonic." "Are you saying that the devil has never tempted these people, and they are not experiencing a spiritual battle for their minds?" I asked somewhat bewildered. The lack of any mental peace is why most people drink and use drugs. At the time, Bob was still attending AA meetings several times a week for his own benefit, and struggled with weight problems. Twenty years later, Bob called our office and asked for help. He said, "You were right. We are in a spiritual battle, and snow I know what it means to be a child of God." One of our staff had taken Bob through the Steps to Freedom. A few months later he died a peaceful man.

The popular Twelve-Step Program began with the Oxford Group, a religious movement popular in the early twentieth century and was originally six steps. It was a Christ-centered Presbyterian program that was bearing fruit. Others took note and wanted to use the program, but didn't want to accept Christ. Eventually six more steps were added and the concept of God was replaced by a "Higher Power" and it ceased being a Christian ministry.

The turbulent sixties ushered in a new era of promiscuity with "free" sex and "free" drugs. License replaced legalism, and the era resulted in a number of Christians needing help to overcome addictive behaviors. At the time the Calvinists and the Armenians were battling each other, and the non-charismatics were battling the charismatics, but very few biblical scholars were tackling the theological issues that dealt with addictive behavior, psychological problems, and spiritual bondage. On the other hand the secular world had come up with many psychological theories and programs, and that is largely where the Christian academic community started from. Trying to "Christianize" secular psychology and secular recovery programs led to syncretism (combining two different forms of beliefs). With the programs came a lot of beliefs and methods that were not consistent with Scripture. What we needed was synergy, a biblical worldview with an understanding how the body and soul function together with God.

Here are my concerns. First, AA participants are encouraged to "work the program, because the program works." There is no program that can set anyone free. The reason the original six steps worked was because of Christ, not because of the program. If Christ is in it, almost any program will work, but apart from Christ we can accomplish nothing that has eternal consequence. Many will object to me saying that, however, because the program has and does save many people's lives. If they had continued drinking and using drugs they would have physically died. But the program cannot save them spiritually; only Christ can do that. The ultimate value is our spiritual life, not our natural life, which we will all lose some day no matter what we do or believe.

It is not my purpose to denigrate other people's programs, because many are doing some fine work. They may, however, bear more fruit if their program includes the life of Christ and is more consistent with the truth of God's word. My purpose is to resource such ministries with a biblical theology of conflict resolution. The real question is, "Can we live a righteous life?" Or do we have to keep sinning? I have spoken at many recovery conferences. When they invite me I say, "I don't want to come and contradict what you are teaching." I then explain what I believe, and to this day they have all said, "That is why we are asking you to come."

A church invited me to speak at their recovery conference, and the director shared his own testimony Sunday morning before I spoke. He said, "I came to this weekend thinking I was a hopeless alcoholic, and would struggle all my life. Now I realize that I am a child of God, and I can be really free in Christ."

Second, secular counselors and therapists know that most presenting problems are symptomatic. So they have developed programs and techniques to get at the root issues. The goal is to develop a trusting relationship with their "clients" (I really don't like that word), so that they will open up and share their inner feelings and best kept secrets. But God already has complete knowledge about that person, so why not include Him in the process?

I have asked conference attendees if they would be willing to share all the "dirt" in their lives, just for the purpose of sharing it. Nobody wants to do that. Then I asked how many would be willing to share all the dirt in their lives for the purpose of gaining some understanding as to *why* they are all screwed up. A few would raise their hands. Some would cautiously raise their hands halfway, but most didn't respond at all. The response is the same all over the world. Most people will not voluntarily submit to secular counseling techniques or secular programs because all they are offering is an explanation of why they are dysfunctional, and then suggest better ways to live with their past. Sadly, such is the state of "Christian" counseling when God is not included in the process.

Finally I asked, "How many would be willing to share all the dirt in their lives for the purpose of resolving it?" Almost every hand went up. The secular world cannot offer complete resolution, because they have no gospel. Their clients are just products of their past, but Christian inquirers are new creations in Christ. God doesn't fix our past. He sets us free from it if we would only repent and believe. No secular therapist will ever suggest that the only means of resolving personal and spiritual conflicts is repentance and faith in God, but it is.

Third, the secular world believes that chemical addiction is an incurable disease. Once an alcoholic (addict), always an alcoholic (addict). That is bad theology that sounds like once a sinner, always a sinner. That is not true either. Once we were sinners, but now we are saints who sin. You can't expect to live a righteous life if your core identity is sin. Blaming it on a disease is supposed to make a person feel better, but for many it absolves them from assuming their responsibility to live a righteous life. Sin is not a disease. Sin is what separates us from God when we are sinners, and sin is what keeps us from an intimate relationship with Him when we become His children. I will concede that some may be predisposed to certain strengths and weaknesses as a result of the fall, but no one is born an alcoholic or homosexual. God created us male and female.

Fourth, AA programs have participants introduce themselves as addicts, alcoholics, co-addicts, and co-alcoholics. Is that really who they are? Shouldn't the Christian say, "Hi, I'm Neil, I'm a child of God who is struggling with a certain flesh pattern, but it is not who I am, and I am learning how to overcome my addictive behavior by the grace of God." Reinforcing a failure identity is counterproductive to becoming complete in Christ.

Fifth, the goal in many recovery programs is sobriety. If abstinence is the goal, then Ephesians 5:18 would read, "Be not drunk with wine, therefore stop drinking." Yet the apostle Paul has a different answer, "Be filled with the Spirit." He also reminds us, "But I say, walk by the Spirit, and you will not carry out the desire of the flesh" (Galatians 5:16 ESV). What happens if alcohol is taken away from someone addicted to it? They become a dry drunk, and will likely be more miserable than they were before. Their means of coping was taken away without resolving their inner conflicts and showing them how they can abide in Christ. Try taking an old bone away from a dog? You will have a dogfight. Try throwing them a steak, and they will spit out the old bone.

Sixth, they talk about dual diagnosis, but in reality there will always be a multiple diagnosis. Addicted people have a poor sense of self-worth; they are depressed, anxious, fearful, ashamed, angry, and bitter. You cannot resolve those issues by simply taking away their drug of choice.

Seventh, most recovery programs, treatment centers, and counseling techniques are not taking into account the reality of the spiritual world. If they live in the United States, most Christian counselors and pastors with secular training don't either. When I was teaching at Talbot, there was an eating disorder clinic close to the school. Most of the clients were Christian undergraduate students at our university. One of them came to see me. After hearing her story I led her through the Steps to Freedom In Christ, and God set her free. She had tried to tell her counselor what her inner struggle was, but was given an assignment to write a paper that answered the question: "Why blaming the devil for my problem was abdicating my responsibility for getting well." I actually agreed with his premise. I would never accept the "devil made me do it," excuse either, but that was not the problem. The real problem was that this counselor had no clue about the student's spiritual battle. Nor did he have any tools by which he could resolve the conflict.

Word got back to the clinic, and other young ladies came to see me. The eating disorder unit closed a few months later. Why do young ladies cut themselves, take laxatives to lose weight, or binge and purge? This doesn't have anything to do with food. It is all about deception. They believe there is evil present within themselves. One young lady was taking seventy-five laxatives a day. While going through the Steps, I said, "This may not make any sense to you, but I encourage you to say after me, 'I renounce taking laxatives as a means of cleansing myself, I trust only in the cleansing work of God.'" As soon as she said that, she broke down and cried for ten minutes. When she regained her composure, I asked, "What were you thinking during that time?" She said, "I can't believe the lies that I have believed." She was a graduate of a fine Christian school. Such problems are not about the lack of intelligence, they are about deception, and even good people can be deceived.

The apostle Paul speaks to this issue in Romans 7:21 (NASB), "I find then the principle that evil is present in me, the one who wants to do good." Paul is not saying that he is evil, but that evil is present within him. Obviously laxative abuse, purging, and cutting oneself will not get rid of the evil. Paul goes on to say, "For I joyfully concur with the law of God in the inner man" (verse 22, NASB). The non-believer doesn't joyfully agree with God, nor do they confess that the law of God is good (verse 16). True Christians living in bondage to lies want to do what is right. The next verse explains where the battle is, "I see a different law in the members of my body, waging war against the law of my mind…" Paul then asks, "Who will set me free from the body of this death?" (verse 24, NASB). Jesus will – if we let Him.

Ninth, those who go into treatment for a chemical addiction seldom get treated for their sexual addiction. I would estimate that 95 per cent of those who are chemically addicted are also sexually addicted, and they inherently know that their sexual addiction will be harder to overcome. So they remain in bondage to that as well. Almost every Christian that I have led through the Steps has had some sexual problem that needed to be resolved. Sexual strongholds are pandemic, which prompted me to write, *Winning the Battle Within: Realistic Steps to Overcome Sexual Strongholds* (Harvest House, 2008).

In preparation for writing the book, I was watching the Sunday evening program, *60 Minutes*, on November 21, 2003. One segment was on "Adult Entertainment," which I didn't particularly care to watch, but I ended up downloading a copy of the report, because I was so astonished by what they said. At that time, in summary:

- $10,000,000,000 was spent every year on adult entertainment and "reputable" industries like General Motors, Marriot Hotels, and Time Warner were cashing in, because the profit margin is so high.

- There were 800 million rentals of adult video tapes and DVDs in video stores.

- In 2002 the porn industry produced 11,000 titles.

- The porn industry employed 12,000 people in California alone.

- 50 per cent of the guests at major hotels were using pay-per-view porn, which accounted for 75 per cent of their video profits.

- Type in the word "sex" in a search engine like Google and you would get 180 million sites.

I sent the above data to our UK office to be put into a syllabus for a conference I'd been asked to do. Steve Goss, our UK director, changed the data after typing the word "sex" into the same search engine. In three years the number had increased from 180 million sites to over 300 million sites. When I sent the manuscript to the publisher they did the same and the number of sites had increased to nearly a billion.

A report from the Center for Disease Control from the year 2000 tells us that:

> *In the United States, more than 65 million people are currently living with an incurable sexually transmitted disease (STD). An additional 15 million people become infected with one or more STDs each year, roughly half of whom contract life-long infections (Cates, 1999).*

David Kyle Foster, the child of a Presbyterian pastor, who gained some fame as an actor, wasn't acting when he doubled as a male prostitute. Life in the gutter finally drove him to Christ, and he has become an advocate for sexual freedom and healing. David had me do several video segments for some productions he was doing. According to David, if there are sixteen people sitting in one pew in any church, two will be struggling with sexual identity. He is not suggesting that one in eight is gay; he is saying that one in eight has some mental confusion about their sexual orientation. Four of the sixteen people are sexual abuse victims. The "official" estimate is: one out of every four women and one out of every seven men, but that is based only on what is reported, which makes the more likely scenario to be one out of every three women and one out of every four men.

In the same pew of sixteen people an additional four will struggle with some form of sexual addiction, and that is true of every pew in your church. Those numbers would also be true if every person sitting in the pew was a pastor, who is a human being like the rest of us. I surveyed the student body of a good conservative seminary and found out that 60 per cent of the male student body was presently feeling some sexual guilt. Of that group, 50 per cent said they would take an elective that would train and help students and others overcome sexual bondage for credit if it were offered. Would you care to guess what happened when I showed the results to the Dean?

Nothing happened at the seminary, so these students will go into ministry with that burden. While searching for answers, two passages from Scripture came to my mind. The first was Romans, 6:11–13 (ESV), "So you also must consider yourselves dead to sin and alive to God in Christ Jesus. Let not sin therefore reign in your mortal bodies, to make you obey their passions. Do not present your members to sin as instruments for unrighteousness, but present yourselves to God as those who have been brought from death to life, and your members to God as instruments for righteousness." If we commit a sexual sin, we use our bodies as instruments of unrighteousness, and we allow sin to reign in our mortal bodies. Confession alone will not resolve this conflict.

The other passage is 1 Corinthians 6:15–17, "Do you not know that your bodies are members of Christ? Shall I then take the members of Christ and make them members of a prostitute? Never! Or do you not know that he who is joined to a prostitute becomes one body with her? For as it is written, 'The two will become one flesh.' But he who is joined to the Lord becomes one spirit with Him." I can't explain it, but I know that when two have sex outside the will of God, a bonding takes place. Obviously there will be an inner conflict if a Christian has become one flesh with another person outside marriage, and at the same time become one spirit with the Lord. While going through the Steps inquirers pray, asking the Lord to reveal to their minds every sexual use of their bodies as instruments of unrighteousness, and God does. As each experience comes to their mind, they repent by saying, "I renounce having sex with [person], and I ask you to break that bond, sexually, mentally, and emotionally."

Perhaps this is why the apostle Paul used such strong language in Romans 12:1 (ESV), "I appeal to you therefore, brothers, by the mercies of God, to present your bodies as a living sacrifice, holy and acceptable to God, which is your spiritual worship." Once the inquirer has broken the immoral bond with another person, they can be spiritually bonded to God. Then they can obey the next verse that instructs us not to be conformed to this world any longer, but to be transformed by the renewing of our minds. Trying to win the battle for our minds without genuine repentance is almost impossible. But when there is mental peace, transformation starts taking place.

Finally, discipleship counseling goes beyond Cognitive Behavioral Therapy, which is the most accepted method of counseling in the United States, both secular and religious. The concept is simple. People are doing what they are doing and feeling what they are feeling, because of what they have chosen to think and/or believe. Therefore, if you want to change what people are doing and feeling, what should you change? What they believe. Repentance literally means a change of mind. But is that enough?

I was asked to teach a Doctor of Ministry class at Regent University. Dr. Fernando Garzon called me in advance and asked if I would be willing to conduct research on the participating students. He wanted to see how effective our approach was in resolving their personal problems. The class was a one-week intensive on Discipleship Counseling lasting nine hours every day for five days.

Over forty students ended up taking the class, which also included Doctor of Psychology Students and Master of Divinity students. Near the end of the class the students were led through the Steps to Freedom. Keep in mind that these students did not represent the general population: they were all committed Christians doing graduate work. In addition, most students take a class to fulfill a degree requirement and hopefully gain some insight to enhance their ministry, and not necessarily to have their life changed. But I agreed to do the research. Dr. Garzon told me later that he hadn't expected me to do it. I said, "If what I am doing is not bearing fruit, I would want to know that."

The students took pretests Monday morning at the beginning of the class, and Friday afternoon at the end of the class. They also took the same tests three weeks later. Every scale was statistically significant: the class showed clear positive changes in overcoming depression, fear, anxiety and anger. Dr. Garzon reported the results in a paper that was published by the *Journal of Psychology and Theology*, which is published by Rosemead Graduate School of Psychology at Biola University. They asked Dr. Garzon how I could explain such results. In other words, what was I doing beyond Cognitive Behavioral Therapy? That is a fair question. Their point was: I taught them the truth, they believed the truth, and the truth set them free. End of story, or is it?

When Dr. Garzon related the question to me I said that three issues come to mind. First, cognitive therapy is practiced by Christian and secular therapists and when used effectively it does bring about brief changes in mood and behavior, but it doesn't change who the person is. Christians have the advantage because they have divinely inspired truth to work with. However, even if you use the words of Christ in Cognitive Behavioral Therapy without the life of Christ, you will not be very effective in producing lasting change. When I say the "life of Christ" I am not referring to the physical manifestation of God 2,000 years ago, I am talking about the eternal life of Christ that defines every believer. Jesus is not our helper. He is our life.

Second, you will not see the kind of results our ministry typically sees using Cognitive Behavioral Therapy if you don't take into account the reality of the spiritual world. If people are paying attention to deceiving spirits, you cannot resolve that just by submitting to God (see James 4:7). You would have to finish the verse, that is, resist the devil and then he will flee from you.

Third, I am not the Wonderful Counselor. I didn't set that class free, neither did the Steps to Freedom In Christ. Who set them free was God. What set them free was their choice to repent and believe. I believe that Scripture has adequate answers for the mental and emotional problems that encompass the Church today. I have tried my best to show that Christ is the answer and that truth will set us free.

In July of 2010 we had our annual meeting in Chennai, India. Our office in India was celebrating its fifteenth anniversary. After our meetings we offered a Discipleship Counseling conference to the Christian community. The hotel could only accommodate 300 people, so we had to turn some away. We also had to for financial reasons. There is no financial gain for doing conferences in places like India. In reality we had to raise money to cover the expenses. One man we could not turn away was Father Sebastian. Mother Teresa of Calcutta had handpicked him to be the spiritual director of their groups. Father Sebastian had found his identity and freedom in Christ through one of my books. He brought sixteen mothers superior with him to the conference, and they all went through the

Steps to Freedom In Christ. Each one of the nuns oversees one of their charities. Now our office in India makes available *The Steps to Freedom In Christ, Catholic Edition* by Neil T. Anderson with Father Sebastian. The book is essentially the same, but it includes the Apostles' Creed. Father Sebastian travels to all their groups and leads them through the Steps.

After the first day of the conference, another group had put some chairs together in a circle in the front of the room. One of our staff informed me that they were a group of counselors and a psychiatrist who wanted to talk with me when I had time. They were laughing and joking together when I was finally able to meet with them. Their big question was, "Why isn't every counselor using your material?"

From Chennai I went to Sri Lanka. Their civil war had just ended six weeks earlier. The Tamil Tigers had finally been defeated after nearly thirty years. Tamil is the third most common language in India, and the Tiger revolutionaries came from the Indian population living in Sri Lanka. Our Indian director, Isaac Manogarom, was Tamil-speaking and his father, Victor, had been born in Sri Lanka. So I wasn't sure what to expect.

We passed through sixteen military checkpoints on our way from the airport to the hotel. That Sunday I spoke at the People's Church, which is the largest church in Sri Lanka. They asked me to speak on forgiveness and reconciliation. The first service I was translated into Tamil. The second service was in English, and the third service was translated into the native language of Sri Lanka. They had obvious political tensions within their own church body. The next two days I did a discipleship counseling conference for 900 Christian leaders. What a privilege to carry the message of reconciliation around the world. What a privilege to see God set captives free and bind up the broken-hearted right in front of you. What a privilege to be an instrument in God's hand. What a privilege to be a child of God. What a privilege it has been all these years to serve God, and to suffer shame for His name. Thank You Jesus.

Afterword

Discipleship Counseling Training

Nancy is 50 years old and exhibits many maladaptive psychological, physical, and spiritual symptoms. She feels lethargic about life, struggles with interpersonal relationships at home, and doesn't seem to connect at church. She makes an appointment to see her doctor who discovers that her blood sugar levels are high. In spite of the fact that Nancy is at least fifty pounds overweight, the doctor doesn't question her about her eating habits or lack of exercise. Her spiritual condition isn't considered as an option for treatment, so the doctor gives Nancy a written prescription for an oral diabetes medication to treat her pre-diabetic symptoms.

Nancy dutifully takes her medication and makes an appointment to see her pastor. He listens patiently about her struggle with depression and family problems. He asks about her prayer and devotional life, which are virtually non-existent. He suggests that she spend more time with God on a daily basis and recommends a good book to partially replace her television "addiction." Meanwhile she continues her same eating habits and tries to improve her spiritual disciplines.

The medication for her pre-diabetic condition gives her chronic indigestion, so she starts taking an H2 blocker like Tagamet, which reduces her digestive symptoms, but now her stomach acid, which was low to begin with, is practically non-existent. Consequently, she's not digesting food as well, which reduces her nutritional input. The medication also puts more stress on her kidneys and her estrogen level is low, which results in a urinary tract infection.

Her doctor puts Nancy on antibiotics for her urinary tract infection, but that lowers her immune system and kills all the beneficial bacteria in her colon. The result is a bad case of the flu, which she can't seem to overcome, and she has constant gas from a colon imbalance.

She starts taking antihistamines for a sinus infection, and her doctor recommends a hysterectomy to solve her urinary tract problem. The advice seems logical, so Nancy has the surgery and starts taking synthetic hormones, which make her feel depressed and weepy. She sees a psychiatrist who writes out a prescription for Prozac to treat her depression. Nancy is now taking a diabetic medicine, an H2 blocker, antihistamines, synthetic hormones, and Prozac. She's exhausted all the time, mentally flaky, emotionally withdrawn, and waiting for the next health problem to hit, and it will!

Let's start over again. Instead of seeing her doctor, Nancy decides to confide with a good friend at church. The friend asks about her past and her present lifestyle. The encourager senses that Nancy has some unresolved personal and spiritual issues and invites her to attend a small group that is going to start a Freedom In Christ Discipleship Class. Nancy's inclination is to decline the offer, because another night out sounds like too much work for someone so exhausted. Her friend reminds her that it would be good for Nancy to get away from family responsibilities once a week and do something for herself for a change.

Reluctantly, she agrees to come to the Bible study. Her friend recognizes that Nancy needs a lifestyle change, and invites Nancy to come with her to the YMCA and start an exercise program that isn't too extreme. She makes a new friend at the Discipleship class who shares how she lost several pounds just by eating smarter. They agree to meet and discuss proper nutrition.

Several months later, Nancy has resolved her personal and spiritual conflicts, found her identity and freedom in Christ, and discovered what it means to be a child of God. With the encouragement of her friend, she has stuck it out at the YMCA and her energy level has increased significantly, due partly to her new eating habits. She has lost 20 pounds and her blood sugar level is normal. She has made some new friends at the YMCA and at the small group Bible study.

Freedom In Christ Ministries seeks to provide a biblical, balanced and holistic answer for life's problems. That includes proper rest, exercise, and diet. We have sought to equip the church with material and training to resolve personal and spiritual conflicts so churches can establish their people alive and free in Christ. There are not enough professional pastors and counselors to help even 5 per cent of the population. The church must equip the saints to do the work of ministry.

The material for training encouragers includes books, study guides (which greatly increase the learning process by helping people personalize and internalize the message) and several series of video- and audiotapes (each series comes with a corresponding syllabus). Trainees receive the most thorough training when they watch the videos, read the books and complete the study guides. We recommend spending two hours a week for sixteen weeks. The material should be presented in the order listed:

Basic Training

Sessions 1–4

Video/audio: "Victory Over the Darkness"
Reading: *Victory Over the Darkness* and Study Guide

Sessions 5–8

Video/audio: "The Bondage Breaker"
Reading: *The Bondage Breaker* and Study Guide

Sessions 9–16

Video/audio: "Discipleship Counseling" and "Helping Others Find Freedom In Christ Video Training Program"
Reading: *Discipleship Counseling*

The book, *Discipleship Counseling*, has further instructions for how to set up a Discipleship Counseling Ministry in your church. We don't want to add to the workload of any pastoral staff, and we aren't: we firmly believe that Discipleship Counseling has the potential to greatly reduce their load and equip the lay person to do the work of ministry.

Core Material

Victory Over the Darkness with study guide, audiobook and DVD (Regal Books, 2000). With over 1,300,000 copies in print, this core book explains who you are in Christ, how to walk by faith in the power of the Holy Spirit, how to be transformed by the renewing of your mind, how to experience emotional freedom, and how to relate to one another in Christ.

The Bondage Breaker with study guide and audiobook (Harvest House Publishers, 2000) and DVD (Regal Books, 2006). With over 1,300,000 copies in print, this book explains spiritual warfare, what our protection is, ways that we are vulnerable, and how we can live a liberated life in Christ.

Breaking Through to Spiritual Maturity (Regal Books, 2000). This curriculum teaches the basic message of Freedom In Christ Ministries.

Discipleship Counseling with DVD (Regal Books, 2003). This book combines the concepts of discipleship and counseling and teaches the practical integration of theology and psychology for helping Christians resolve their personal and spiritual conflicts through repentance and faith in God.

Steps to Freedom In Christ and DVD (Regal Books, 2004). This discipleship counseling tool helps Christians resolve their personal and spiritual conflicts through genuine repentance and faith in God.

Restored (E3 Resources). This book is an expansion of the *Steps To Freedom In Christ*, and offers more explanation and illustrations.

Walking In Freedom (Regal Books, 2008). This book is a 21-day devotional that we use for follow-up after leading someone through the Steps to Freedom.

Freedom In Christ (Monarch Books, 2004 and 2009; Regal Books, 2008). This is a discipleship course for Sunday School classes and small groups. The course comes with a teacher's guide, a student guide and a DVD covering 12 lessons and the Steps to Freedom In Christ. This course is designed to enable new and stagnant believers to resolve personal and spiritual conflicts and be established alive and free in Christ.

The Bondage Breaker DVD Experience (Harvest House, 2011). This is also a discipleship course for Sunday school classes and small groups. It is similar to the one above, but the lessons are 15 minutes instead of 30 minutes.

The Daily Discipler (Regal Books, 2005). This practical systematic theology is a culmination of all of Dr. Anderson's books covering the major doctrines of the Christian faith and the problems Christians face. It is a five-day-a-week, one-year study that will thoroughly ground believers in their faith.

Dr. Anderson's Specialized Books

The Bondage Breaker, The Next Step (Harvest House, 2011). This book has several testimonies of people finding their freedom from all kinds of problems, with commentary by Dr. Anderson. It is an important learning tool for encouragers.

Overcoming Addictive Behavior, with Mike Quarles (Regal Books, 2003). This book explores the path to addition and how a Christian can overcome addictive behaviors.

Overcoming Depression, with Joanne Anderson (Regal Books, 2004). This book explores the nature of depression – which is a body, soul, and spirit problem – and presents a wholistic answer for overcoming this "common cold" of mental illness.

Liberating Prayer, (Harvest House Publishers, 2011). This book helps believers understand the confusion in their minds when the time comes to pray, and why listening in prayer may be more important than talking.

Daily in Christ, with Joanne Anderson (Harvest House Publishers, 2000). This popular daily devotional is also being used by thousands of Internet subscribers every day.

Who I Am in Christ (Regal Books, 2001). In 36 short chapters, this book describes who you are in Christ and how He meets your deepest needs.

Freedom from Addiction, with Mike and Julia Quarles (Regal Books, 1997). Using Mike's testimony, this book explains the nature of chemical addictions and how to overcome them in Christ.

One Day at a Time, with Mike and Julia Quarles (Regal Books, 2000). This devotional helps those who struggle with addictive behaviors and explains how to discover the grace of God on a daily basis.

Freedom from Fear, with Rich Miller (Harvest House Publishers, 1999). This book explains anxiety disorders and how to overcome them.

Extreme Church Makeover, with Charles Mylander (Regal Books, 2006). This book offers guidelines and encouragement for resolving seemingly impossible corporate conflicts in the church and also provides leaders with a primary means for church growth – releasing the power of God in the church.

Experiencing Christ Together, with Charles Mylander (Regal Books, 2006.) This book explains God's divine plan for marriage and the steps that couples can take to resolve their difficulties.

Christ-Centered Therapy, with Dr. Terry and Julie Zuehlke (Zondervan Publishing House, 2000). A textbook explaining the practical integration of theology and psychology for professional counselors.

Getting Anger Under Control, with Rich Miller (Harvest House Publishers, 1999). This book explains the basis for anger and how to control it.

Breaking the Strongholds of Legalism, with Rich Miller and Paul Travis (Harvest House Publishers, 2003). An explanation of legalism and how to overcome it.

Winning the Battle Within, (Harvest House, 2008). This book shares God's standards for sexual conduct, the path to sexual addiction and how to overcome sexual strongholds.

The Path to Reconciliation, (Regal Books, 2008). God has given the church the ministry of reconciliation. This book explains what that is and how it can be accomplished.

For more information or to purchase the above materials contact Freedom In Christ Ministries:

Canada:	freedominchrist@sasktel.net www.ficm.ca
India:	isactara@vsnl.com
Switzerland:	info@freiheitinchristus.ch www.freiheitinchristus.ch
United Kingdom:	info@ficm.org.uk www.ficm.org.uk
United States:	info@ficm.org www.ficm.org